THE BROKEN MIRROR

The Broken Mirror

By O. Bryant Tyndall

Copyright © 2021 O. Bryant Tyndall

All rights reserved.

ISBN: 9798594644397

TITLE: The Broken Mirror
By: O. Bryant Tyndall
Edited by: Angee Costa
Cover Design: 846 Publishing
Copyright 2021

The author has made every effort possible to ensure the accuracy of the information presented in this book. However, the information herein is sold without warranty, either expressed or implied. The author, publisher, nor any dealer or distributor of this book will be held liable for any damages caused either directly or indirectly by the instructions or information contained in this book.

In accordance with the U.S. Copyright Act of 1976, the scanning, uploading, and electronic sharing of any part of this book without the permission of the publisher is unlawful piracy and theft of the author's intellectual property. If you would like to use material from this book (other than for review purposes), prior written permission can be obtained by contacting the author. Thank you for your support of the author's rights.

Notice of Rights: All rights reserved. No part of this book may be reproduced or transmitted in any form by any means, electronic, mechanical, photocopy, recording or other without the prior written permission of the publisher.

Permission: For information on getting permission for reprints and excerpts, contact the author.

DEDICATION

I would like to dedicate this book to my wife (Judy) and our three children (Beth, David and Patrick). You will always be that bright spot in my life. You are perfect in every way. My memories of growing up in Varina and Willow Springs were not always so bright or so perfect. Remember, a pinch of salt always makes the pudding a little sweeter. Thanks for the love, memories, and joy you have given me as your husband and father.

Judy Godwin Tyndall

Beth Wilson

David Tyndall

Patrick Tyndall

ACKNOWLEDGEMENTS

I would like to thank the North Carolina State Library in Raleigh, the Olivia Ramey Local History Library also in Raleigh, the Fuquay-Varina Branch, and the Cameron Village Branch of the Wake County Library Systems.

Also, thanks to the Angier Branch of the Harnett County Library System for their help in confirming references for some of the material in this collection. A special thank you is due to Shirley Simmons, my friend, for her expert guidance through much of this endeavor. I would like to also acknowledge and thank Mrs. Julian Pearce (Edith) and Mrs. Denver Hardman (Ruth) for sharing their unpublished stories and history notes on Willow Springs. Thank you to Willa Adcock for her perseverance and online writing of some of her accounts of her mother and cousins (the Adams sisters) and their recollections of Willow Springs. Also, I wish to thank all the people in Varina, Willow Springs, and Angier, who shared their stories with me in this collection.

Finally, I would like to thank my wife who has been at my side over all these decades while this collection process was underway. She has read these accounts countless times making corrections and suggestions and encouraging me to continue. Her comments have always been constructive and uplifting.

TABLE OF CONTENTS

INTRODUCTION 7

Chapter One – My Willow Springs..11

Chapter Two – Remembering Varina 15

Chapter Three – How It All Happened 23

Chapter Four - Why Write All This Stuff?....................................29

Chapter Five – Memories of Special Places and People 39

Chapter Six – "The Mighty Multiplying Myatts" 63

Chapter Seven – My Story and My Family 69

Chapter Eight – Special People of North Street 87

Chapter Nine – Special People of Willow Springs 97

Chapter Ten – Remembering Some Special Chores.................137

Chapter Eleven- Remembering Strange Events........................151

Chapter Twelve - Remembering the Oddities..........................163

Conclusion 179

About the author 181

FOOTNOTES 183

INTRODUCTION

It has been said everybody has at least one book in them. So, I am guessing this is my one and only shot as it has taken eighty years to write this one. What follows are my stories and my collection of stories from others as they passed through my life in Varina and Willow Springs over these past eighty years.

My story goes something like this. Once there was a little boy in Varina who loved to question, seek, and explore. At a very young age, this little boy came to understand treasures are not always gold or silver. Memories and recollections of memories were just as rare and precious as jewels. It was then that this little boy started his quest to collect those cherished memories.

From the age of nine, he was always looking for long lost treasure; perhaps a pirate's hoard. He never found it. However, one day this little boy discovered an old barn broken by time and nestled in the piney woods of Varina. When he mustered the nerve to enter, he found that it was filled with many things: old newsprint and old furniture—treasures long forgotten. Not the gold he had hoped for. Among the many things he found was an old mirror dusty and shattered, the result of time and neglect. He thought as he gazed into that broken mirror about the people who may have looked in that very same mirror years ago. Who were they? What had they seen? What joys had they celebrated? What losses had they grieved?

It was then and there that his quest began to collect stories from folks along North Street, his Varina childhood home. He talked to folks in Willow Springs, his home as an adult. More importantly, he wrote down many of their accounts. Just maybe this little collection book of that little boy will stir in you some of your sweet memories. Don't forget to write them down.

That little boy spent almost all his childhood in Varina. Those were happy days. He played all the childhood games, attended all the birthday parties. He had a handful of best friends and mile high dreams for the rest of his life. He rode his Donald Duck bicycle around the countryside in Varina exploring every field and farm, questioning everyone he met. Then, as today, he possessed an engaging humor that views life as more than a problem to be solved. It is an opportunity to be enjoyed. That love of life was enhanced by being around people and collecting their life stories.

On the outside, he had all the trappings of a normal life, but he was hiding a deep dark secret. His family was poor and he could do nothing to change it. His poverty was not that of a starving or homeless child. He had food on the table, indoor plumbing, and a roof over his head, but not much more.

Looking back at days gone by stirred within that young fellow a passion to know more. He wanted to listen, learn, and write those stories down preserving them for all time. At first glance, these conversations seemed ordinary and uneventful. The folks he talked to often drifted from subject to subject. But, like fine wine that grows sweeter with time, they revealed more than he ever expected.

Memories are those little golden nuggets lodged deep in the mother lode of your mind. Every day of our lives, we add more nuggets to the mother lode. The only enemy is time. A tombstone in Oakwood Cemetery in Raleigh bears the name of Rev. Isaac McKendree Pittenger and simply reads "lived 29,212 days," a somber reminder to us all—our days and our memories are already numbered.

That young fellow arranged his recollection book into twelve chapters. He recalls memories of his life in Willow Springs and Varina. What follows is how it all happened and why it was all written down. He explores some special places around Willow Springs and Varina and attempts to explain the multitude of Myatts in Willow Springs

He will never forget the neighbors along North Street and the memories created with friends in Willow Springs. Somehow, the work and fun got done long before the help of all those modern electronics. In the midst of it all, special events were celebrated. At times, some odd and inexplicable things occurred.

It is all captured on the coming pages with the hope that it will give you a chuckle or a reason to pause and ponder.

Many other folks along the way have provided help in this endeavor and also added their memories to this collection. If you are reading this now, you are most likely my friend or at least an acquaintance. This book is a collection of those memories of my childhood in Varina and my adult life in Willow Springs. Oh, by the way, that little boy was me.

Chapter One – My Willow Springs

I moved to Willow Springs in 1963 and spent my adult life here. When I got out here, there were just a few deer hiding in the sparse forest but seldom ever seen. Today, they are everywhere crossing newly carved highways, causing many automobile accidents, and eating everyone's vegetable gardens. I also remember geese flying over Willow Springs heading North or South as the season dictated. Today, they stay year-round and make a mess on everyone's lawn. Finally, let us not forget those dreaded fire ants. Who opened that box and released them on our community?

I assume these are just natural changes and I will have to adjust. Change is, after all, the basis of life.

What about the changes man has made out here? That is a harder adjustment. In 1910, there were fifteen family surnames living in this dark corner of southern Wake County. "The entire population of Middle Creek Township in 1910 was 2,213 while the adjacent Panther Branch Township boasted only 1,687."[1] These same families established homesteads in the unincorporated crossroad communities of Willow Springs, Myatts Mill, and Mount Pleasant. According to K. Todd Johnson and Elizabeth Reid Murray, "Willow Springs was a small railroad-stop community near the Wake and Harnett County line south of Raleigh."

The community took its name from a water source and a Primitive Baptist Church dating from 1826. When the Cape Fear and Northern railroad laid tracks through there in 1899, a post office was established at Willow Spring (no "s" on the end). William B. Temple was named postmaster. J. Lewis Rowland succeeded him in 1919, followed by William I. Rowland who served thirty years beginning 1920. J. W. Blalock and sons operated a cotton gin and K. B. Johnson operated one of his many sawmills (circa 1902).

Other Early twentieth century merchants included L. D. Adams, J. D. Love, J. W. Rowland, and John D. Johnson. By 1896, a school was built. In 1919, this one-room, one-teacher school reported an average daily attendance of thirty-three students out of the sixty-eight students enrolled."[2]

By 1926, a new school was built on the same site consolidating and enlarging the student enrollment by taking all the students from the schools at Mount Pleasant and Southern Side. Shortly thereafter, both schools were closed.

In her book, The Historic Architecture of Wake County, Kelly A. Lally suggested "The Willow Springs community in southern Wake County has its roots in an early nineteenth century village known as Bank's Quarter, at the center of which was the Willow Springs Primitive Baptist Church organized in 1825. The first Willow Springs church building was located near the springs for which it was named, about a mile north of the site of the current church and cemetery."[3]

"The North Carolina Gazette" described Willow Springs "as a community in Wake County settled about 1800 and named for the Weeping Willows in the vicinity. A Post Office was established about 1899."[4]

The Willow Springs I know and love today extends from Willow Springs Service Center (my ground zero) northwest to the Hilltop community at highway 401, west to highway 55 at the Five Points community, (known earlier as Old Shops) then east to the Johnson County line at highway 50 and south to the Harnett County line near Angier. I have not looked lately, but I think the Fuquay-Varina planning zone has laid claim to the rest of the real estate in southern Wake County.

Just think: Willow Springs could have been a real city with a town hall, several strip malls, traffic jams, and a bypass around it all called Myatt parkway, if only we had acted eighty years sooner.

While reading this book you may notice when I make reference to Willow Springs, I am also including with it the communities of Myatt's Mill, and Mount Pleasant. Only the community of Mount Pleasant is located in the Panther Branch Township while Willow Springs and Myatt's Mill are in Middle Creek Township. To me and many of the old-time residents out here, they are all the same community.

Don't worry too much about the townships and their border-line locations. They are not as important today as they were when created back in 1868 as tax districts. Today, the postal system identified as "Willow Spring" includes parts of three counties, five telephone exchanges, and eleven rural routes with rural post stations totaling 8,000. The distance from west to east is about thirty miles.

By 2020, folks living in those same communities represented every state in the Union and several foreign countries. Indeed, a lot has changed. Indeed, a lot has remained the same. Every community in Wake County, regardless of its size, has seen something like the changes swirling around Willow Springs in the recent past. Have you been to 'historic downtown Varina lately? That little sleepy community has also changed. The traffic on any afternoon in the historic village can make travelers sorry to have chosen that route. Holly Springs, Clayton, and Apex are also experiencing these growing pains. However, they seem to have better roads to deal with the traffic.

Someone needed to stop, sit back, and reflect on the way things used to be before leaping head-first and blindly into the future. Someone needed to write it all down. I think that job has been assigned to me. John Hope Franklin, a famous North Carolina historian, reminds us of one of Santayana's quotes from one of his many aphorisms, "Those who forget the past are condemned to repeat it." [5]

Daniel Boorstin once said:

> *"Trying to plan for the future without a sense of the past is like unto planting cut flowers."* [6]

All I expect to do in this endeavor is to catch a fading glimpse of some of the wonderful people as they brushed past my life under the shade of those lovely Willows and in the case of my Varina days, under the shadow and watchful eye of Annie Akins. She owned our house and most of the other houses along Varina's North Street in the 1940s. She lived atop a little hill along East Broad Street. There she had a lofty view of everything and everybody along North Street.

While I have not used this material in any direct quotes, the microfiche reel for Fellowship Presbyterian Church of Willow Springs has provided a valuable baseline for remembering some of these folks and faces living in Willow Springs first as Presbyterians and later as Baptists. Discovering that reel was a great day for me. It took a lot of effort and money to get it in my possession. It records names and events as they unfolded in that little church and community. Those records span a distance of time between 1913-1961. I have greatly enjoyed reading this reel as it brings to life names and faces long since departed from this world.[7]

Chapter Two – Remembering Varina

The greater Varina I knew as a child included the outlying communities of Wilbon (possibly named after an early property owner, S. G. Wilbon and wife Edna). They granted right-of-way for rail tracks through their 71-acre farm resulting in a depot and later a post office before 1932. Thanks to attorney John Adcock for this Wilbon information. John's grandfather, John C., opened a store on or near the Wilbon property. Also, in my memory and associated with Varina are the communities of Needmore, Lewis Parish's Fruit stand (later known as Mack's village), and Five Points (known earlier as Old Shops). Setting exact boundary limits for all these unincorporated areas is difficult and is more of an art than science.

My recollections of Varina and her days gone by take me up and down those busy sidewalks—a journey I repeated on a recent trip down memory lane (December 2018). Seventy years ago, that was my playground. It was my front yard. I ran up and down those sidewalks daily becoming intimately familiar with every crack in that pavement and how to jump over them. "Now, as the timber resources slowly dwindled in the Varina communities and the saw mills went out of business, bright leaf tobacco production eclipsed the lumber industry." That was a big event for the economy of Varina. Fuquay Springs was also "Johnny on the spot" and got its first tobacco warehouse in 1908. "Walter H. Aikens opened the first warehouse in Southern Wake County. With no banks in town at that time, he paid the farmers from his pocket." [8] To tell you the truth, I did not pay much attention to all these economic events at the time. Some folks called it Varina Station or Union Station—for me it was just Varina.

My Varina recollections, along with those of other Varina folks, provide a backward glance into my Varina days. The book, A History of Fuquay-Varina, especially chapters five and eight also provided great help in recalling Varina and her bygone days. My memories of Varina and Broad Street are not just the places but also many of the faces.[9]

Ben Franklin once said:

"Write something worth reading or do something worth writing about."

Well, Ben, I am not sure if I have done either one of those things. But here is my best shot. These memories are of folks who lived, died, and impacted my life, both in Willow Springs and in Varina. Where there are people, there will be records of their deeds. It is all those little bits in the middle that I wanted to hear, see, and write about, not just the sad moss-ladened tombstones capturing only the date of their births and deaths. It is that little dash in the middle that interests me.

The town of Fuquay Springs had two "tobacco redrying plants" and that helped the economy of Varina. It was those redrying plants that provided the last steps in the long process for tobacco from field to factory. Those plants were responsible for packing and shipping those golden leaves to factories where they were made into the best cigarettes the world ever tasted. Employment in the redrying plants added yet another boost to Varina and Fuquay's economy.[10]

Back then I knew every merchant in Varina and they knew me. My memories of Varina started around 1946 when my family moved back to Varina after living out the war years (1941-1945) in Norfolk, Virginia. Today, as I walk along Broad Street passing a brewery, a bakery, lots of quaint shops with sidewalk dining and people everywhere, I am stirred by memories of days gone by. My thoughts wander back to a time when life was not in such a hurry. Today, the air on Broad Street is electric with excited young folks all on the move at a quick pace. Seventy years ago, those same sidewalks were heavy with the humidity of a hot July day. No one seemed to be in a hurry to come or to go. Time dragged by like a wet dog. I thought it would always be that way. I never thought about change. Boy, was I wrong!

"Generally, those folks who lived north of the Methodist Church on Main Street and down Ennis Street to the Presbyterian Church considered themselves to live in Varina proper. All the farm families to the north and to the west along "Durham and Southern Railroad" also considered themselves as residents of Varina. Consequently, loyalty to Varina became palpable."[11]

The community of Varina was never really a town until 1963 when it merged with the incorporated town of Fuquay Springs. The two communities became one town, Fuquay-Varina ("A Dash Better"). Before the merger, the Varina community had a little business district known as Broad Street. Most of the Broad Street properties were owned by the family of B. G. Ennis. With the coming of the railroads (1910), a depot was built and named Varina Station. The rail tracks crossed North, South, East, and West offering destinations anywhere in the United States from my little Varina, though you might have a few train changes along the way. The depot is still around and is now the site of the "Aviator." John Eual Brown was appointed first railroad agent and later his daughter, Katherine, assumed that duty until 1977.[12]

The Browns built a "Sears Kit" home located at the west end of Broad Street after clearing the trees to extend the road. With the passage of time, several more houses and a few businesses were built extending Broad Street westward to the intersection with highway 55. The last name "Brown" will forever be linked to the railroads around Varina. (John and Katherine as railroad agents, wife Beatrice as office manager, daughter Elizabeth as part-time summer help, and son Olan as freight manager).

About 1911, Dr. J. Alexander Sexton's subdivision map showed properties to be developed behind Varina Supply, a business selling farm supplies and most everything else. Varina Supply was operated by Newton H. Hopson and J. Herbert Akins. Varina Supply operated from 1924 until 1965.[13] After 1965, the building held several businesses and is now (2018) a sports bar. Dr. Sexton also named the street he developed after the city of Durham. Durham Street intersects highway 55 near Wake Chapel Christian Church.[14]

Facing east down Broad Street, there was a cotton gin across from the home of Herbert and Annie Akins. East of the gin was a feed mill operated first by the Wheeler family and later by George Francis Sr. I would like to thank Shirley Simmons and Willa Adcock who have so graciously helped me. Their research coupled with my recollections provide a few clear glances looking back at Varina.[15]

Remembering Varina takes me back to some really happy times. Of course, all was not play. There were some sad and uncertain times too, and yes, I have written about them also. I am happy to report there were more happy times than sad ones.

Collecting memories sweet and bitter, means recalling the tragic events that happened in my life. Sure, there were hardships and, from my view, I faced them, overcame them, and promptly forgot them. I take fierce pride in my heritage. I am proud of my humble beginnings and grateful for the folks around me back then and now.

We lived on North Street, post number 605 to be exact, and just one block from Broad Street. Broad Street was neither broad nor long: its west boundary stopped about where Stephens Hardware was. The east boundary stopped about where the old Cotton farm was. So, you might say that would place me squarely in the middle of the wrong side of the tracks. Varina folks back in the forties and fifties really believed there were two sides to the railroad tracks, and Varina was, for sure, on the wrong side. Louise

Meadows, who lived next door to the Tyndalls, was a die-hard believer in the "wrong side of the tracks theory." To make her points clear, she would always say "do you remember at the annual Christmas parades?" She would then remark that the high school marching band never played a single Merry Christmas tune until they reached the city limits of Fuquay Springs. They only used Broad Street as a staging area. She also said the Christmas decorations for Broad Street were never as pretty as those for Fuquay's Main Street.

I loved Louise Meadows. She was like a second mother to me. However, she firmly believed those things, and it was useless to argue with her over those points. She also said that at the Farmers Day Parade, usually held about mid-September, only the cheap candy was thrown out to the bystanders in lowly Varina, while the good stuff was reserved for the folks along the parade route in Fuquay Springs. I don't think there is a way to ever prove her claims, but it did make for lively back-fence conversations. North Street was not paved until the late 1950s.

One of the fun things the young boys did after each summer rain shower was to dam up the ditches creating large pools of water along North Street. By the next day, the water was gone, but I have great memories of making those grand Hoover Dams. Mrs. Annie Akins from the top of the hill cast a shadow over our small street. We lived under her careful, watchful eyes. She did not like our little Hoover dams and often let us know it.

In 1910 the little unincorporated community of Varina had only 200 souls claiming Varina as their residence. With the coming of the railroad, a patch of land across from the Depot started the downtown proper. Between 1910 and 1930, building lots were laid off and purchased by several people. With the coming of the railroad, the Great Depression, the stock market crash, and the dust bowl, the building lots changed hands several times as fortunes were made and lost. Lots behind Varina Supply Store (Herbert Akins' store) were purchased and developed by Dr. J. Alexander Sexton circa 1914. There have been so many changes made to the

Broad Street business district in these ensuing years that the changes are almost too many to recount.

The name "Varina" has a stable and romantic history. It probably relates to a time at the start of the Civil War in 1861, when a letter-writing relationship was established between James Deveraux "Squire" Ballentine, a young man from Fuquay Springs and confederate enlistee and a young lady named Virginia Ayers from Cumberland County. Virginia wrote letters to him under the pseudonym "Varina." Young ladies of that time when writing to a soldier did not dare use their real names to a man they had never seen or been properly introduced to. At war's end, the two met in person and married. From the marriage forward, "Squire" addressed his young bride only by her pseudonym, "Varina." Later he made application for a post office and named it "Varina" in her honor. It has been suggested she may have taken the name Varina after the wife of Jefferson Davis, President of the Confederacy.

The remains of Virginia Ayers and Squire Ballentine now rest at Oakwood Cemetery in Raleigh and her tombstone resides at the Fuquay-Varina museum. You will have to visit the museum to get the rest of that story. The name "Ballentine" will forever be linked to the community of Varina.

For the purpose of recounting my memories of Varina, I am picking the year 1951. I was ten years old and we were still living at 605 North Street only one block off Broad Street. On Sunday afternoons, I would roller skate up and down those paved sidewalks for endless hours. My dog, Rusty, ran alongside me never getting tired. I think he wanted to be with me no matter what I was doing. On a few occasions (usually Sunday afternoons), my friends and I would fly our homemade kites along Broad Street. We could access the roof of most of the buildings along Broad Street from the back stairs leading up to the apartment of Phillip and Michael Kannon. The Kannons ran a clothing store on the ground floor below.

The kites were simple to make. It only took two small lightweight sticks overlapped and wired together forming a cross. String was then looped at each of the four points. Newspapers were cut to fit the frame and were glued over the string. The glue was made from flour and water forming a stiff paste. The last part assembled, and the most important, was the tail made from strips of old cloth. The kites were simple to construct, cheap to make, and easy to fly. We would fly the kites on Sundays and leave them to fly overnight. The lucky kite still flying the next morning was the winner. The merchants probably did not like to see all the crashed kites and string across Broad Street, but they never complained, at least not to me.

From my house, it was a short walk over to Varina Supply Store operated by Herbert Akins and Mr. N. H. Hopson. These men were on my paper route (The Raleigh Times) and they shared one newspaper between them. That was a cheap trick they used to avoid buying two papers. In reality, they could probably have bought the entire publishing company. The Varina Supply Store was a two-story brick building with upstairs apartments for rent. In 1951, Will and Alma Foster lived up there. Will Foster was my grandmother's brother and a constable for Wake County. Next to the Varina Supply store was a one-story building where Wilton Shoals and his wife Ruby ran a dry-cleaning business. Later, they moved the business out to 401 and changed the name to Tops Cleaners. Crossing back over the railroad tracks and back to Broad Street, the building on the west end of Broad was the Varina Post Office operated by Jewel Stephenson. My memory of this post office is not clear. I think that office closed about 1951 and reopened on the East end of Broad Street, next door to Poe's Red and White Grocery Store. Margaret Hall and Helen Honeycutt worked at the new location.

Next to the west end post office was Stephens Hardware store operated by Mr. Isaac Stephens. He was also on my paper route, but I delivered his paper to his Sears Kit home address on Ennis Street. Next to Stephens Hardware store was the Bank of Varina. I am told the Bank of Varina was located further east down Broad Street, but in 1951 it was beside Stephen's hardware store. Now crossing Ransdell Road and facing east on the corner was the Thomas Drug store operated by the Thomas brothers, Willy and John. Next to the Thomas Drug Store was the Varina Barber Shop. Above the drug store and barber shop were apartments for rent. There were stairs leading up to the apartments from Broad Street. There were also steps leading to the apartments on the back side.

The next store front was Creative Crafts, a business operated by A. D. Averette and, in later years, by one of his sons. Continuing east was Alice Bullock's Meat Market. I remember this store well. She kept live chickens out back. Next came Poe's Grocery (store # 1) followed by Carolina Feed operated by Russell Goss. As I recall, Mr. Goss sat on a feed bag at the front of his store greeting everyone who passed by. Next to Carolina Feed was the Varina Theater, Wrenn's Insurance Agency, and Kannon's Clothing store. The Kannons lived upstairs over the store. Mrs. Kannon kept live goats and sheep out back in a small enclosure. Mrs. Kannon also made and shared many Syrian dishes with everyone on North Street. Next was Poe's Grocery (number 1).

The last two store fronts were Cotton's Furniture and Parker's Furniture. These last two fronts were one business originally called the Varina Hotel (circa 1927). Crossing Stewart Street was Weaver Brothers Auto Dealership (later to become known as Poe's Red and White (store #2) operating from 1954-1970) and the east side Post Office. My thanks go out again to Shirley Mudge Hayes, Shirley Tanner Simmons, and Willa Akins Adcock for sharing their information with me as it relates to some of the Varina downtown.[16]

Chapter Three – How It All Happened

Why would anyone attempt such a laborious collecting and writing project as this? The answer may surprise you. The following pages may help you understand why this project was created. The inspiration happened a long time ago. Tucked away at the edge of the piney woods of Varina, I discovered an old house foundation—an old barn out back and an old broken mirror in that barn (circa 1947). That discovery set in motion a desire to write something about those people who may have lived in that old house, walked about that old barn, and may have even looked into that very mirror.

At that time, I had no idea that my adult life would be spent in Willow Springs. That is why these recollections have two locations.

As a young boy, my greatest adventures (and I had many of them), were the solo bicycle trips I took on my new Donald Duck bicycle to old places around Varina. I pretended I was a great explorer searching for buried treasure. I had two rules: never enter a property with "no trespassing signage" and never take souvenirs. On one such occasion, I discovered that old barn still standing, but sadly leaning. I finally mustered the courage and entered. The barn was filled with many wonderful treasures. Wonderful treasures are not always gold and silver as I was soon to realize. I imagined that what I was feeling was the same as Howard Carter felt as he opened King Tutankhamen's tomb back in Egypt in 1922.

Before me were spread many faded boxes, old newspapers, and broken furniture all blanketed with dust. Among the treasures, the old mirror framed in wood caught my eye. The mirror had long since been broken and lay in many pieces on the dirty plank floor.

As I rubbed the old mirror with my coat sleeve, I could see the large pieces contained etchings and perhaps lettering. With only a little polish, the etching became beautifully clear. It was fashioned of swirls making a beautiful border along the broken edges of that mirror. Other chards of the glass were more reluctant to give up their secrets.

Some of the pieces were gone—never to be seen again. Determined to learn more, I laid the pieces out like a giant jigsaw puzzle on that sagging floor. Somehow, I knew that I was about to experience a touchstone moment in my life. I stared into the glass and wondered about the people who once lived here and perhaps looked into this very same mirror.

After rubbing the shards a bit longer, some gave up their design quickly while other pieces refused all my efforts. I left the old barn and my puzzle later that day. But I returned many times to my old and secret treasures. I continued to polish the chards and search for the missing pieces. I think it was then that I knew someday I wanted to write something about the events of the people who may have lived in that old Varina house. My mind filled with questions. What was Christmas like for the inhabitants many years ago? Did they experience tragedy? What joys did they know? Did they marry? What could they tell me about the great wars they survived? Could they share some sage advice with me?

For a long time, I thought I was the only one on the planet that loved to discover and explore these old places. To my surprise and joy, I read an article about Michelle Bower who had similar thoughts and love for these old places. Check out her Facebook page site: "Abandoned Homes of North Carolina." [17]

Recently, I was watching a PBS program, "My Home NC," in which Heather Burgiss interviewed Watson Brown. Mr. Brown, like myself, loved to drive around North Carolina searching for and taking pictures of old houses and barns. Mr. Brown said the pictures awakened memories for him and perhaps other folks. It sure did for me. My thanks go out to both Michelle Bower and Watson Brown for keeping memories alive.

Many folks left snapshots of their lives before they departed this earth. Many saved old letters and ledger books. Their deeds are recorded in dusty, old public records. I learned about their lives by reading old newspaper clippings. I see them in the photographs. Their voices can still be heard decades after their passing.

Recently, I attended my class of 1960 Fuquay Springs High School reunion. We were encouraged to bring old photos. It was a nice gesture, and we had fun looking at the photos. I was a bit sad, though; I had no pictures to share because my folks did not have a camera. Family pictures were something never on their radar. It was a luxury we just could not afford. When I looked over other classmates' pictures, I was reminded of that broken mirror. Some have the pictures and the proof of their younger days. I was not so lucky. That made me even more determined to look back, collect, and write about what I found. Where or how I would do all this only became clear to me many years later.

Over the years, tragedies struck my little family. In 1947, my mother went away to a sanatorium for treatment of Tuberculosis, a dreaded word for many folks at the time. It was a difficult season for our family. Later, in 1957, my Dad had a stroke. He suffered for ten more years, spending most of it in a hospital bed in the front bedroom at our rented house on North Street. Dad and I were not close as father and son should be. His illness only caused us to grow further apart as he could not talk during much of this time. As I recall, he cried a lot and for no particular reason. With no income, we quickly became a family dependent on "welfare," as it was called in those days, and the kindness of strangers.

My return trips to explore that old barn became fewer as I struggled to help my family with more pressing matters. I became too busy with the "here and now" to think much about the "there and then." But I never forgot that old barn and that old broken mirror. I always planned to return to that adventure, but I never did. Over the years, I lost that Donald Duck bicycle but never lost my desire to find out more about the "there and then."[18]

After college, marriage, the Navy, a career in State Government and three children, I found myself and my own little family living in Willow Springs. I quickly fell in love with that little unincorporated crossroads community.

With renewed vigor, and with my wife, Judy, and all three children in tow, I returned to my passion of looking for old houses and barns to explore and memories to collect and write about. This time, my explorations were centered in Willow Springs. Many Sunday afternoons would find us looking for old abandoned farmhouses.

"Have you ever wondered what life was like for the folks that once lived here?" I would ask Judy and the kids. If they did not answer quickly, I would always tell them what I thought.

When the children became adults, we had many laughs around the dining room table recalling those Sunday afternoon trips and some which became weekend adventures.

"Dad never took us to the new places with green lawns," my children would say. "We only got to see old broken-down houses, dirt roads and weed-infested lawns. There was a time when brown road signs pointed the way to historical attractions. Dad knew that meant free admission. Dad would research the attraction we were set to visit. He always knew more than the tour guide, and was quick to let that fact be known."

After many years, I did return to that first old barn back in Varina. Sadly, the contractor's bulldozer had removed all traces to make way for a new subdivision. I was sad to see it go, but I was not discouraged in my quest to continue to look for other old houses, barns, rich life stories, other broken mirrors, and better polish to reveal the secrets they held.

Our lives and those around us are much like that old mirror back in Varina. The best we can hope for as life's curtain is draping low is to have roots set deep and standards held high with family by your side, a fist full of friends, thousands of memories, and someone waiting to hear all of them.

It is my hope now to polish up some of those special memories involving my friends, my family, and our times at my second home in Willow Springs and my first home, Varina. It has been my desire to write these stories for my own joy and perhaps to bring to future generations an account of some of the past. I hope readers whose families have lived here for generations, as well as those more recently arrived, may find that my collective writings will increase their appreciation for the rich history of Varina and Willow Springs and all their fascinating people.

This book is a collection of remembrances mixed with a little research. This is my unofficial and always-to-be incomplete history of Willow Springs, Myatt's Mill, Mount Pleasant, Panther Branch Township, and a little reflection of my early days back in Varina. I will look into some of the special places, special people, special times, and special happenings. A few ghost stories, some odd facts, and some old-time sayings are in the mix just to keep everyone on their toes. Happy memories are out there somewhere. The real trick is to find them within yourself first and then share them with others.

This book has been put together by jogging the memories of some of those precious people. There are references to folks and events in my hometown of Varina. This endeavor is an attempt to chronicle events, times, and flavors of these people. I seek not to capture the drama of a place, more appropriately it is memories of a time long gone by but, for me, never forgotten. The timeline is held generally between 1913 and 1963 with a few exceptions. The place is set among the sandy soil and Willow trees and along 'the dirt roads of Varina. Even with great care, errors will be made in transferring this material from worn, handwritten records, then photographed to microfiche reels, and finally transcribed to this document. "Often the data was not legible or complete, leading to inferences and assumptions that were not always correct. I alone accept the responsibility and plead for corrections from readers who discover errors."[19]

Chapter Four - Why Write All This Stuff?

Each day, thousands of newcomers to Willow Springs and Varina identify their location only in terms of where they live in proximity to the closest exit ramp on I-40 in their morning drive and evening return. They quickly learn the fastest way out each morning as they commute to work centers in our research triangle and beyond. I am thankful for the newcomers and happy for their success. I welcome them to my area. They bring a fresh new perspective to our lives. There is room for all of us.

My joy now is to share with them happenings and days past. My fondness for living here is authentic and sincere. I truly love the people of Varina, that sleepy little community, until its merger with Fuquay Springs in 1963, and Willow Springs, another sleepy little community at the eastern edge of Middle Creek Township.

I am especially fond of connecting them together in the complex tapestry that is their life and my joy. Studying the history of this part of the county is fun. It is filled with oddities. Panther Branch Township is a township without a town. That does sound odd, but it is true. There is only Willow Springs, Myatt's Mill, and Mount Pleasant; those little unincorporated communities in southern Wake County first settled in the early 1800s and named for the weeping willow trees that grew so freely around the springs that bubbled up in the vicinity. My friends, Ruth Holland Hardman and Edith Pearce, were also interested in Willow Springs history. The three of us often shared our notes and information. Sadly, they have both passed now before their findings could be published. I owe them a great debt of thanks for sharing with me. Ruth Hardman, Bob Sheets, Peggy Dean, and myself shared a carpool to and from State Government in Raleigh. Edith (Mrs. Julian Pearce) was a member of our senior's group at Fellowship Baptist Church. We all had many discussions about writing a history of the area.

In their notes, they recalled the first landmark for the area to be Willow Springs Primitive Baptist Church. In 1972, "Willow Springs was a small rural village with mail routes covering 157 miles and providing mail service to 2300 families. The mail routes covered parts of three counties and several telephone exchanges. Today that same mail route is much larger. The second landmark is Panther Branch, a little creek basin that rises in Southern Wake County and flows into Middle Creek." [20]

Today there are no panthers, at least no real ones. There are accounts of folks killing panthers (1900-1912) and claiming the reward offered by the County Government. Stories still abound of the Willow Springs' wild cats and other dreaded beasts living along the banks of our lakes and swamps. As for the branch, it is now but a wet spot just north of Panther Lake. Middle, Swift, and Black Creeks all flow into the Cape Fear or Neuse river basins, just two of the 17 river basins located in North Carolina.

Newcomers to this area seldom reflect on the weather-beaten tobacco barns, the farmsteads, and cemeteries as they rush by on their way back to their little patch of paradise on their cul-de-sac each evening. Our old tobacco barns do not shout their history to them as they speed past. A gentle flutter of the almighty kudzu vine is all that moves. And yet our gentle rolling hills are alive with memories. Our little country stores, plank churches, peaceful cemeteries, and vacant houses all gently ask to be heard. They all have countless stories to tell. The well-groomed cemeteries whisper soft words of wars, of personal sorrows, of great depressions, of epidemics, and of hope after this life. After all is said and done, the graves are the gateway to eternity. We just need to slowly walk the cemetery paths and back roads on a warm spring afternoon and listen to their stories of wonder.

My new friend, Michael Doyle Boyette penned these words in 1991 in his salute, "Ode to a Tobacco Barn."[21] In it, he expresses my tender affection for these old structures so much better than I.

> Standing alone in the evening sky,
> Pigeons from your gables fly,
> And twining up your weathered side,
> Vines of green, decay to hide,
>
> Tobacco barn, so old and forlorn,
> On your tier poles, our harvest born,
> [Leaves of gold] now are seldom seen,
> Once routinely hung from your wind beam.
>
> From lantern light to lantern light,
> During hellish days and steamy nights,
> Under your top and roundabout,
> We filled you up and took you out.
>
> Ten cent oil was it not,
> That got your insides fiery hot?
> First to yellow and then no doubt,
> Those golden leaves to kill out.
>
> On to better things and newer,
> Now that labor's so much fewer,
> It seems to be your solemn luck,
> That today it's all done in bulk.
>
> Decay and rot, your end is near,
> Will you be standing another year?
> Good-by to you and those times well past,
> Secure in our memory till the very last.

These words chosen by Michael Boyette and selected for use in his poem, may suggest that only a few will understand his words. Just talk to anyone living here in the "Bright Leaf Tobacco Belt" and older than 75. We can interpret all this for you. As for me, I understand it all too well. I lived through some of those hellish days and steamy nights. I can still smell the tobacco gum that stuck to your hands and clothes like blackened glue. I don't know which was worse—the sticky tar gum or the lye soap required to remove it. I remember those summer days when 4:00 am came mighty early bringing with it the chore of taking out a barn of cured tobacco before starting to refill the same barn with green plants. Even in the summer when the fields were wet with morning dew, the primed leaves were cold to the touch. Our clothes and skin were soon wet through and through. There was much to do even before the long day started. Someone had to get the mules harnessed before the sunshine. Seems to me that was my job along with my friend, Terry Overby. I was about ten years old then. The mules were not always ready for another long day of hard work, much less the harness.

Terry and I worked for his father, Billy Overby. The Overbys were tenant farmers on the Cotton family farm just at the eastern edge of Varina. The Overbys were kind, honest, loving people trying their very best to make a living from the soft but often unforgiving sandy soil of Varina. Billy's wife, Louise, always fixed a big breakfast for her family. This was served after the cured barn was emptied and before the long day started for gathering the green tobacco leaves. While I was not a family member, she always made sure I had meat and biscuits.

Why would anyone go to all this trouble to collect and assemble all this material? I have thought about this question for many years. I can only say the people in southern Wake County and that little white plank church accepted me in 1963 and have allowed me to call this place home. William Faulkner once said "the past is never dead. It is not even past."[22]

Yet another quote someone said many years ago:

"History is prophecy looking backward."

That is how I also feel about exploring the past. To me, it is alive. To me, it is a puzzle waiting for assembly. To me, it connects us all. Our likenesses far exceeded our differences. We were and are all a part of a connected bond—some by bloodlines, some by friendship, and some by proximity. Events happening in 1913 affect and mold events that happened in 1963.

There is one rule you must follow out here. In Willow Springs, everyone is connected, most often by bloodlines crossing and re-crossing. You have to be careful what you say and to whom you say it as you may be talking about someone's cousin. At some point in-between, there are little glimpses of the life in the middle and that is what I want to explore and record. I want only to say how thankful I am to be a part of this little settlement here on the eastern edge of Middle Creek Township.

Many families make-up the population out here, and it is tempting to include them all; but I will leave the genealogy and tracing of family roots to someone else. The Myatts are the one exception. They are everywhere, and I will have more to say about them later. I will also talk more about the core families along Varina's North Street.

By 1963, the little white plank church, which I will call my first church, was Baptist with rich Presbyterian roots and was the site of my marriage on July 6, 1963—the last one performed in that building. Soon after, the little white plank church, like my little old barn and that broken mirror back in Varina, met their final fate to make way for bigger and better things to come. Just up the hill, a larger Baptist church building soon rose out of this rich farmland. This structure I will call the middle church and it witnessed the marriages of two of my children. The church cemetery holds the remains of my grandchild, Sarah Abigail Tyndall, infant daughter of David and Sabrina Tyndall, my son and daughter-in-law. These fertile, gentle hills are my home now. My roots in this area run deep. These people, some mentioned in this writing project, are my social friends, my church family, and my biological family. They are threads woven into the fabric of my life. These people and these places helped me find my wife, raise a family, manage a career, and not so quietly retire. They have seen me grow up and out, and they are endearingly special.

I did say I wrote this collection of memories for my own pleasure, and that is true. I still hope someday someone will be looking for information on a special family member, or a special place, a special event, or just a special memory and will be directed my way. Maybe someone in the future will say, "There was an old man down on Bud Lipscomb Road who wrote down some stuff. Maybe he can help you. He wrote down lots of stuff and over several decades but could never make up his mind what to call it or how to arrange it."

I am thrilled to have completed the journey of writing all these things down. Someone else must decide if the effort was worth the time. "Remembering Varina and Willow Springs" is not a test for dementia. It is not an official history of a church or building or group of people living under these Willows or along North Street in Varina. It is much more. It is the stories of men, women, times and places with a little white plank church and a Varina street weaving a beautiful patchwork quilt. It is going to take a lot of questioning, polishing, patching, and wondering how things really were between 1913 and 1963 here under these Willows and along North Street. Nothing has been done to intentionally mislead or misstate the facts. This collection is now, and will forever be, a work in progress.

Recorded herein are some of those gold and silver treasures I uncovered while moving this project forward. Some may think it dull to just sit and listen to folks talk about whatever crosses their minds. But after writing down what was said, you will be amazed at what is revealed and the depth of their revelations. What they believe to be important is also important to me. Perhaps others may enjoy reading their accounts.

Memories are ephemeral; they don't stay in your conscience mind forever. They fade like a glorious sunset. There are no pockets in funeral shrouds nor are there trailer hitches on a long gray hearse.

When we leave this earth, we will go as we came, unadorned and taking nothing with us. We will be leaving only the memories of the good times and the bad. No one will ever know these memories, sweet or bitter, unless they are told to someone or, better still, written down. I was absolutely sure I would never forget those treasured conversations of yesteryear with folks in Varina and Willow Springs. I was wrong. Who knew asking such simple questions as: "Tell me about your life at age 10 or 20." That was enough to spark the rich and complex conversations I enjoyed. I asked them to tell me about their marriages or their recollections of Pearl Harbor and December 7, 1941. I asked where they were when World War II ended? Who knew all this would open so many treasure troves of memories? You think you will never forget the details, but it happens. We tend in life to forget more than we remember. The simple solution is to just write it down.

After you read this chapter take a few minutes each day and write down some of the memories you have collected over your life. Include memories you may think are not important. They may turn out to be golden nuggets to your friends and family later on after you and I are gone.

Here are a few tips that have helped me along the way:
- Keep pen and paper around.
  If you are prepared, you can capture the memories that pop into your mind or jot down information you collect.
- Do not wait too long to write your findings.
  If you wait, you are likely to forget and potentially lose an important fact.
- From time to time go back and ask for clarification.
  Something may come to mind for the people you interview that they can add to what they have already shared.

Photographs are especially important when telling the stories of the past. As we all get a little older, we will collect photographs of our loved ones. Sure, you will always know who these people were. But when you are no longer around will your family know these people? The solution to this problem is to take some time to write the names and perhaps the date on the reverse side of the picture. Pull out those photographs often and show them to your children and grandchildren. Never judge or belittle the information you are receiving. Seek out the oldest members of your family and with a pleasant face-to-face conversation, harvest the bounty of their knowledge. Physical photos fade over time or can get lost or damaged. So be sure to preserve a digital copy of your pictures. If you don't know how to do it, visit your local library or office supply store. They will be glad to help you.

Sometimes it helps to have your tape recorder nearby. You will need to be careful with the recorder. Some folks don't like to talk freely when it is running. You can tape your recollection at a later time. But don't wait too long.

I have always enjoyed talking to folks almost as much as looking for those old houses, barns, and broken mirrors. I love listening to stories of things and times gone by. Talking in a comfortable setting is just like exploring; instead of finding treasures, you find memories. Sweet memories uncluttered by today's complicated lifestyles where you must be sure everything said and done is politically correct. These memories are dear to the hearts of our older citizens and to me. These folks truly enjoy reflecting on days and times now fading into history. I fear there is a time coming when we will only talk to computers, voice mail, e-mail, and those dreaded text messages. These new inventions are stealing live conversation and those wonderful face-to-face encounters. Soon we may only know how to communicate digitally using the fewest words possible. Are we losing an art form here?

The folks I have talked with over these years are very sharp when it comes to times and events of days in the past. While they may have difficulty recalling where they left their car keys, they are quite clear on people, dates, and places back in time. They are walking encyclopedias. They can quickly polish up some of those dim memories for you. Tucked away in their minds are nuggets of knowledge that they are happy to share with anyone who will take the time to listen. The key to obtaining all this information is just a matter of a kind word and a keen ear. One of those wise seniors, Mrs. Vaughn Phillips back in Varina, once gave me some good advice.

She said:

> *"Son, you only learn when you listen. Silence allows the information you hear to come in and to be sorted out in your mind. Talking allows the information you think you may know to come out. While you are talking, you are not learning, but just repeating what you have already learned. Listening allows you to fill your head with knowledge that in later times you can allow out or just stay wisely quiet and renew yourself."*

The noted writer, Pearl S. Buck, expanded on Mrs. Phillip's thought when she once said:

> *"Inside myself is a place where I live quiet and all alone and that is where I renew my springs that never dry up."*[23]

Mrs. Pearl S. Buck and Mrs. Phillips could have been next-door neighbors, at least in giving wise advice. Another great thing once said by Mrs. Phillips was this:

> *"God gave us two ears and only one mouth."*

That wise lady was on to something. How astute of those folks to know all that and to share it with me. When I find memories in written letters and diaries, I am especially thankful. Not only have these people taken the time to remember the past, but they have written it down for future generations to reflect on. Horton Cooper, a writer of histories in western North Carolina, once recollected:

> *"Where there is human life there are interesting events. People are born, live, work, plan, accomplish, laugh, weep, love, marry, die and are buried."*[24]

Yet, only the births and deaths are usually recorded on those moss-laden tombstones. What a shame to miss all that good stuff in between. Thus, I resigned myself to share a bit of that good stuff. Some of these interviews were done by me; many were done by others and later told to me. I am eternally thankful for all those who took the time and effort to record, transcribe, write, and rewrite some of these accounts. I want to give them all just recognition for their efforts and generosity for allowing me to share them here in this project. Each story is like a little jewel of a person's heart: spontaneous, free, and uncluttered. I will continue to look for all the missing pieces between those cold, sad tombstones.

The following are in no particular order. I start with my memories of some very special places in Varina and in Willow Springs. Most of these places are gone now and, with the passage of time, so too will be the sweet memories I have of those places.

Recollecting not only covers special people but may also bring up special places that stir up memories and are worth recording. Such are the special places mentioned here. If you really think about it, you too may recall other places and your pleasant thoughts of similar places. Memories, be it of special people, special times or places fade with each passing year. It is true we are living in an age of information. Knowledge is out there just for the taking. Unfortunately, memories often do not stand the test of time. Consider these gems of places around Varina and Willow Springs as we smile, laugh, and look back.

Chapter Five – Memories of Special Places and People

Willow Springs and "The Pines"
I really do not know where to start with this unusual place. I know it did exist and since this section is about special places, people, and times, it must be the right time to share it. If you head east along highway 42 just after it separates from highway 55 at Five Points, you come to an area known then as "The Pines." In the late 1950s and perhaps earlier, this was just a loop, a dirt path leading into some scrub pine trees. Over the years, many cars driving along that path created a dirt road. Young boys, and sometimes their girlfriends, who visited "the Pines" often had their own parking place. It could be called assigned parking I suppose. They were just private places along the path suitable for long stays and for undisturbed lovers' conversations and perhaps even a little star gazing. Often the parked cars were many in number. This was a special place during those warm, dark spring and summer evenings. The frequent users had their reserved parking spots and everyone else knew to stay out. The place was well known to everyone living in Fuquay Springs and Willow Springs. Now in 2020, "The Pines" is just a memory. The Johnson Concrete plant now resides in that general area. The pine trees and those long-forgotten parkers are all history now except for those of us who dare to write and to remember.

Varina and Thomas Drug Store
As a very young boy, I loved to visit Thomas Drug Store. I can't say when it came into existence. Occasionally, my Grandmother Gertrude Foster Honeycutt would give me a special treat when I would fake feeling bad and she allowed me to skip school that day. She would walk to Thomas Drug Store where she would buy me a milkshake and a grilled ham sandwich with potato chips. I will

never forget how good it was. Often, later in the day, one of the Thomas Brothers, Willy or John, would call to see how I was feeling. In the summertime, my little gang of friends would visit the drug store on those scorching summer days for a banana split. It was three scoops of ice cream topped with chocolate, butterscotch, and strawberry syrup in a long boat-shaped glass dish. Of course, the banana was split and placed into the dish. Nuts were extra. The banana split cost only twenty-five cents and we would sit and eat it under the cool of an overhead ceiling fan. The little tables were glass top with a metal frame with chairs that were all metal. Did you know one of the Thomas brothers invented a cough syrup? Later I was told only Mr. Willy was a real pharmacist. John was his partner and pharmacist assistant. Little did I or the Thomas brothers realize those were some of my happiest days growing up in Varina. Just above the drug store were several apartments where I lived for a short time after I was born.

Willow Springs and "The Stagecoach Inn"
The Inn was located about 100 yards off the old Stage Road sometimes called the old Federal Road at the intersection of John Adams Road. The Inn (now removed) served as the post office, stables, and overnight room and board for guests. Stage Road provided a route between Raleigh and Benson, a distance of about forty miles. In the 1950s, the Inn was a two-story building with a bell attached atop a wood pole to sound the arrival of the coaches and perhaps the diners. Like the "Pines," the Inn was used for other purposes in the 50s and 60s. The Inn and several adjacent buildings were disassembled in the early 1960s. The story I got is that a man from California approached Mr. T. Floyd Adams who was the current owner of the property. The man bought the building and took it apart board by board. It was suggested to me that the building was put together with wood pegs, making it a unique example of the craftsmanship skills of that time.

After numbering each board, the entire structure was shipped out to California. It took five flatbed trucks to haul it away. No one is quite sure why he wanted the building or whatever happened to it, but he must have wanted it badly to have gone to such effort and expense. Some of the foundation rocks are still visible today. My good friend, Fred Fish, suggested the building was taken down by Willie York, a Raleigh urban developer, and the wood was used to build his Raleigh residence. There is some evidence suggesting a house was owned by Mark and Mary Myatt, grandparents to William Alfred Myatt. The building was approximately 1,000 feet south of the future site of the Frank and Mary Smith House (now owned by Fred and Frances Fish). The Myatt house functioned as an Inn during the late eighteenth and early nineteenth centuries. Just for the record, Mark and Mary Myatt moved to the Willow Springs area in the 1780s. They could be the first of many Myatts in our area. The land grant maps dating back to 1720 suggest that Mark Myatt was granted several parcels of land arcing around southern Wake County.

In 1958 several high school friends and I from the Fuquay area, usually up to no good, would drive out to the Inn. We would make our way up the steps at the old structure where we waited for nightfall when, like clockwork, the cars came. We gave everyone plenty of time to settle down. Then, in the pitch dark, we climbed out the window on the 2nd floor and threw rocks at the big dinner bell just outside the house. The parked cars began to make a hasty exit. On one of those occasions, a young lady from Willow Springs, in her haste to leave, left her coat on the ground. The next Monday all the boys involved in the bell ringing took her coat to the school office "lost and found department." The school secretary reported over the school public address system: "A coat had been found over the weekend and could be claimed at the school office." We waited around the corner of the office, and pretty soon the girl showed up and claimed the coat. We never told her where we found the coat. There was no doubt she knew.

Angier and the Gators, Gourds and Johnson's Gardens
It may take some effort to keep this story moving forward but just trust me it sure makes for some great memories. It was the summer of 1958. I was working at Poe's Red and White Grocery Store in downtown Varina. I knew most of the customers by name and I made it a point to learn something about each one of them. Many of those folks have now passed. Still, some of them will

always be a part of those great memory pieces stored away in my mind. That was the case with Mary and Marvin Johnson.

The two of them still shine bright in my memory. They always made a point to talk to me about high school, my grades, and my college plans. The Johnsons were the only people I ever told about my desire to go to Campbell College, and they always encouraged me to pursue that dream. During the summer of 1962, I was a sophomore at Campbell College. I was still at Poe's Red and White (only on weekends), and by now I was the assistant meat cutter. There were only two of us working in the meat department. Mr. Johnson called me his master butcher. He said I could work wonders cutting up a whole chicken. Once, when he was expecting guests for Sunday dinner, he came by Poe's Red and White to get two chickens for his special event. He asked if I could cut up the chickens to fry. I had never done that before, but I said yes without a minute of hesitation. A few days later Mr. and Mrs. Johnson came by the store to tell me how much fun the guests had trying to guess what part of the chicken they were eating. We all had a good laugh. I never told Mr. Poe or anyone else. I realize this section is about the gourds, gators, and gardens and I am getting to that.

Are there alligators in Angier? You better believe at least one was there. Well, it was about this time that Mr. Johnson told me he had an alligator in the pond by his house on highway 55 near Angier. My job was to save the beef bones and meat scraps for the alligator. I thought that was pretty cool. I always made sure the gator had plenty to eat. Each week, the Johnsons would give me a progress report on the only alligator I ever knew to exist in Harnett County. I will never forget the Johnsons and the story of their exotic pet. I am still encouraged by their kind words and guidance.

In 2013, I spoke with a co-worker of mine at the Department of Insurance. Somehow that alligator story came up in the conversation. My friend said she too remembered that Angier alligator. I thought it interesting to hear her version of the story. According to Marcia Kelly, her father, Lynn Senter Mann, was given the baby alligator by his older brother after a trip to Florida.

Her dad was a teenager at the time. We are not sure of the timeline, but at some point (we think it was when her daddy went to college) he passed the gator to Leonidas Judd Betts, Jr. (Lee was her cousin and Daddy's nephew) who was 5 years his junior. Lee kept the alligator in an old well enclosure at the home they were living in off Highway 55 near where the Johnson home place once stood. The alligator continued to grow. He eventually got too big for the small well enclosure and needed to be in more water. Lee's Dad, Leonidas J. Betts, Sr. (dubbed Uncle Lonnie), contacted Mr. Johnson to see if he would allow the gator a good home in the Johnson's pond. Mr. Johnson was happy to allow this as he was having problems with folks trespassing around his pond and bog gardens. Mr. Johnson was a kind soul and would not hurt anyone, so perhaps the sight of that alligator would stop the trespassers in their tracks. So, the alligator went to live in the Johnson's pond.

When Marcia was little, her daddy would take her to the pond to feed the alligator. She recalls patting the top of the water at the edge of the pond to "call" the alligator. He would come up and eat the hotdogs and loaf bread she had brought for it. The alligator lived a very long time but met his demise when an unknown person shot and killed him (probably a trespasser). Marcia believes she was a young adult when this happened but can't exactly recall when it happened. "I know there was a newspaper article about it when he was killed. It may have been in the Harnett County News."

Thanks, Marcia, for that little walk down memory lane.

Now let's talk gourds. According to Mr. Johnson, who had a wealth of information about many subjects, gourds are among the oldest crop in the world. They are cousins of the squash family. Their hard-shell variety can last for centuries. I have one of their gourds, now past 50 years old, still in pristine condition. The Johnsons are gone but the gourd museum is still here and well worth the free visit. Since Mr. Johnson's death in 2003, the collection was left to Kennebec Baptist Church. It is now housed in the Angier Municipal Building at 28 North Raleigh Street.

My beloved Willow Springs and Varina are blessed to have folks like the Johnsons as a part of those glimpses back in time and memory.

Mary Lee McMillian wrote an article about the Johnsons and their humble home and lakeside gardens. The Johnsons not only created a museum to honor the lowly gourds of the world and offered a home to a misplaced alligator, but they created gardens to show off the beauty of nature.

"The garden collection contained tons of petrified wood, old mill stones, an authentic Indian canoe and sculptured driftwood. The Johnsons collected not for themselves but to share all this beauty with anyone passing by. The garden pathway led down a sloping hill past countless wildflowers, mountain laurel, and Japanese iris. At the garden entrance was a plaque which read: "If you have a mind at peace, a heart that cannot harden, go find a door that opens wide upon a lovely garden."

The woodland trail widened past columbine, bloodroot, rue, anemone, and wild geraniums. Last, but not least, were the beautiful bog gardens at the end of the trail alive with pitcher plants, Venus fly traps, locelia, wild lilies, and orchids. The trail ended at the antique marble statue of Saint Francis, the patron saint of gardens and flowers" and perhaps Angier's lonely alligator.[25]

Not much of the garden exists today. Sadly, it met its fate at the end of a contractor's bulldozer. In just a few hours, the garden was gone to make way for a new subdivision. It is much like that old song: "You don't always know what you got til you lose it. You pave paradise and put in a parking lot." Although the alligator and the flowers are gone, my memory of these beautiful places and the Johnsons still remains in that special place of my heart.

Varina: H & H Grill

This personal memory takes me back to my teenage years and retains a truly special place in the hearts of folks from both Varina and Willow Springs. It was much more than an early fast-food store. It was a legendary place where memories were made. It was the place to meet after your date. The grill had an old floor-model jukebox and for twenty-five cents you could listen to three songs. In 1956, Fats Domino's "Blueberry Hill" led the pop chart. Located three miles north of Varina along highway 15A (later to be known as 401), it boasted of the "Finest Food Anywhere." The grill had a unique system of food delivery. You just drove in the parking lot and waited in your car. Shortly, a young lady, sometimes in a pink poodle skirt, and sometimes called a "car hop" came out with a menu. Your order was prepared and delivered back to your car in record time. The food rested on a tray custom-made to fit on your car door window (driver's side).

I have to admit those hot dogs were the best ever and cost only 15 cents. Sometimes we ordered our hot dogs "all the way." Let me explain. My information comes straight from the expert short order cooks around southern Wake County. The hot dog and the bun were steamed separately. The hot dog was usually red in color and probably not very nutritious. The brand I remember was "Jesse Jones." If you ordered your dog with coleslaw only, it was ordered "one dog in the grass." If you ordered your dog with slaw and mustard it translated to "one dog in the grass, painted." If you added catsup and onions to your dog it was translated to "one dog in the grass painted, bleeding, and crying." That is what was meant by "all the way."

The short order dictionary, created by yours truly, is endless with its terms. The Grill telephone was 232-R Varina N.C. (check out that short phone number). Mr. and Mrs. J. P. Honeycutt operated the grill. This information was taken from an ad in the 1955 Willow Springs Flicker School Annual.[26] The H & H grill was quite the place to be and be seen in 1958. I know this first-hand.

Varina: "The Cairo Drive-In
This very special place was located four miles north of Varina along highway 401 (then 15A). It was named by K. B. Johnson to celebrate his travels to Egypt. Before it closed in 1970, it was the last surviving outdoor theater in Wake County. I remember with fondness those Tuesday night free shows (about 1956). Everyone turned out for the showing even if the show was a repeat. As a teenager, we had fun visiting everyone in their cars. As I recall, the Bullock family operated the drive-in. Mrs. Bullock made the best-ever popcorn and gave many free samples. "X" rated movies were never shown as folks driving along the highway might get a glimpse and get distracted. On hot summer nights, we would all sit on the ground and watch the movie. The free shows are history along with the drive-in. Today there is a large apartment complex (The Marquee) on that site (2020). The newcomers got the apartments and the liquor store, but I got the memories.

Varina: The Gold Leaf Warehouse
I lived only two houses up from the Gold Leaf Warehouse. Everyone on North Street was interested in the opening day prices for the now cured, graded, and artfully tied bundles of the golden leaf. When, at long last, the harvest was complete, the farmers took their crop to the market where it was sold. Opening day at the warehouses in Varina and Fuquay Springs was big business. You could feel an air of excitement and anticipation as first sale days grew near. There was a great sense of pride in the finished product. Most tobacco was sold in an open auction system with the buyers and sellers all walking along the lines of baskets. The pungent aroma of the cured tobacco filled the air in the warehouse and traveled all the way up North Street. The farmers jokingly said it was the smell of money. At eight years old, it all looked very unorganized to me. However, to the auctioneers and buyers, it made perfect sense.

The merchants in Fuquay Springs and Varina thanked the farmers by having a day set aside called "Farmer's Day." There were always parades, BBQ suppers for the barn help, and street dances for all. The farmer's day parade in August 1956 was one of the best days of my life. I rode my new Donald Duck bicycle in the parade as I waved at everyone and threw candy to the children along the streets. Did I mention I saved a full bag for myself? I guess a little confession is good for the soul.

The Gold Leaf Warehouse, through the years, has made an incalculable contribution to the growth and well-being of North Carolina, especially in Varina and Willow Springs. Today, it is just another one of those sweet memories lodged deep in my mind.

"As part of a federal farm program that began during the Great Depression, attempts were made to stabilize pricing of agricultural commodities. Most tobacco grown in the U.S. fell under these price supports and production control systems. Under this program, a majority of growers agree via referendum to accept USDA set acreage and marketing quotas. In return for the restrictions, the growers were guaranteed a minimum price per pound." [27]

By the 1970s all these methods of growing and curing were changing. Bulk barns replaced the curing barns. Those precious leaves that brought such pride and good prices in the 1950s are now bulk cured, thrown into large burlap sheets, and trucked away to market. It is a little sad to me that the same families who grew the golden leaf in the 50s are now waiting for the final federal buyout details. It is somewhat like a death in the family. I know this had to come to pass. I also now know tobacco is harmful to the users. Tobacco farmers were proud people living simple lives in Varina, Fuquay Springs, and Willow Springs and command my greatest respect. They did not know they were raising and selling a harmful substance.

Willow Springs and Varina: Her Rivers, Rails and Roads

The Neuse and Cape Fear Rivers form the two river basins nearest to Varina and Willow Springs. Today, they are both too shallow to allow heavy waterway traffic into southern Wake County. This discouraging fact of our topography is one of the reasons for our area being slow to develop. In earlier times, these rivers allowed boat traffic from the coastal regions to Fayetteville along the Cape Fear and Smithfield along the Neuse. Silt buildup over the years is one of the guilty culprits. One of the topographic high points between these two watersheds is located near the D. H. Fish place along Bud Lipscomb Road. Standing atop this point and looking North over the old Myatt's Mill pond headwaters (now called Panther Lake), the valley opens and reaches all the way to highway 42. It is a beautiful sight on a crisp winter day.

"European and African settlers slowly made their way to Wake County in search of fertile river bottomlands. Many settled for lands along Middle, Swift, and Black creeks. Operating between 1772 to 1800 Rogers Ferry at Wake Crossroads provided a two-way ferry service to folks crossing the Neuse River. After payment of a small toll, the persons and wagons crossed. The power was provided by mules." The ferry trip allowed people and products to move quickly from eastern Wake County to central and Western Wake."[28]

"While a lack of deep water ports slowed development to southern Wake County, the fertile Cape Fear valley did produce large straight pine trees, leading to the creation of the tar, pitch, and turpentine industries bringing wealth to the Willow Springs and other nearby communities in those early years. Beginning in the 1840s railroad construction provided local farmers and sawmills with links to important regional and northern markets. Later those same trees were harvested with local sawmills moving lumber by rail over the entire country." [29]

Some of the finest homes in Boston and New York were built using lumber from Willow Springs.

"The Native Americans passing through southern Wake County believed the waterways were of such importance that they felled trees pointing in the direction of the Neuse and Cape Fear rivers. The remains of some of those fallen trees are still visible today. They provided a clear signage for others to follow."[30]

The creeks of importance for Panther Branch Township and Middle Creek Township were Middle, Swift, Terrible, and Black. When Black Creek was dammed late in the 18th century, it created Myatt's Mill Pond. Further downstream, Black Creek's flowing waters provided power to another mill owned by Hurley Dupree. Terrible creek, so named because of its ease to flood after heavy rainfalls, also formed one of the township's water features.

The community of Willow Springs is described "as a railroad stop community near the Wake-Harnett County Line taking its name from a water source and a Primitive Baptist church dating from 1826. When the railroad and post office arrived in 1899 the community began to grow. When that Willow Spring post office was established (note there was no "s" on the end), William B. Temple was named postmaster."[31]

Much of the following information on the trains in Willow Springs has been provided from the notes created by Edith Pearce and Ruth Hardman. They said: "Much of Wake County had rail service before 1860 but not to Willow Springs. It was not until Mr. John Alliston Mills began building his line in 1899 through Willow Springs that rail service appeared."[32]

Mr. Mills was a heroic figure around southern Wake County. He was born on a farm between Fuquay Springs and Holly Springs.

Miss Ruth Johnson is quoted as saying: "Mr. Mills rose from a humble position with sheer force of character, an indomitable energy, and superior executive ability. He was destined to success." (This sounds to me like Miss Johnson has been reading too many superman comics.)

She recounted that during a flood on the Cape Fear River, Mr. Mills contrived to save the railroad bridge at Lillington by anchoring it with loaded freight cars. It worked. The bridge is still standing though not in use today.[33] Pearce and Hardman also said, "In the beginning, Mills' venture into Willow Springs was a lumber train, but later it handled freight of all kinds. A passenger car was added allowing one trip a day. People coming to the Primitive Baptist Church meetings at Willow Springs would use this passenger train and they were picked up by church members. These train passengers, many of which were tobacco farmers, soon realized the potential for tobacco in this area and quickly moved their families here from many areas, especially Granville County and along the Carolina- Virginia state line." These areas were hit hard by a disease of tobacco called "the Granville wilt." This wilting disease affected the tobacco roots and their ability to mature. The disease reached its peak about 1910 to 1913. The sandy soil around southern Wake County attracted many families to our area. After the Willow Springs Depot closed (circa 1939), Fuquay Springs got the passenger travelers, thanks in part to the healing waters. With the loss of the passenger train, a big chunk of the Willow Springs' economy was gone too. Downtown Varina soon picked up the slack and boasted a fine Hotel serving the needs of many tobacco buyers, and the Blanchard Hotel in Fuquay Springs provided meals and lodging to folks coming to Fuquay Springs for its disease-healing spring waters. Folks called the process "the taking of the waters." The average stay was at least an overnight event. The Varina Hotel later became the site of two furniture stores, Cotton's and Parker's. Today (2021) that location houses a restaurant. The passenger service to Willow Springs and Fuquay Springs was discontinued completely by 1940.

"By May of 1909, rails along the Crepe Myrtle lanes of Angier, N. C. marked the last rail laid and the last spike driven in what we know today as the Durham and Southern Railroad. At that time, it was a little more than a tramway leading from Apex in western Wake County to the Jake Williams farm in Harnett County near the present site of downtown Angier. The little engine powered by lightwood-knots with black smoke puffing appeared like a fire eating monster from the Piney Woods. According to accounts recorded in Voices of Yesteryear a History of Angier, this little railroad was first known as the Cape Fear and Northern Railroad. The purpose of this railroad was to haul lumber and logs. The rails ran along the ridge lines dividing the waters of the Cape Fear and the Neuse. Before the rails arrived, a booming business was ongoing extracting tar and pitch for use in the turpentine industry. As the trees were bled and hacked, (terms used in the 1900s for extraction of pine sap) they were just waiting for the ax. It was the rails that carried the cut trees to the many sawmills operating in the area. Jonathan Cicero Angier owned a lumber plant in Cary, North Carolina. It was Mr. Angier who conceived the idea of building a railroad along the pine ridge from Apex to Harnett County and Mr. Jake Williams's farm."[34]

"Mr. Angier worked tirelessly to build that rail and is the namesake for the town of Angier. Jake Williams holds the title of Father of the City. Jonathan Cicero Angier died in Durham in 1911. Jake Williams died in 1912 and is buried in the Angier. These men were true pioneers of our area." [35]

Paved roads, like so many other things in Willow Springs, were equally slow coming to the area. Many early accounts of our history indicate farmers always kept a team of mules on hand to pull wagons from the sticky mud. To some of those hard-pressed farmers, it was a joy and much-needed source of extra income. I am not sure if the mule teams shared their joy.

"There is an account about 1900 of a horse-drawn carriage wagon taking three hours each way to travel between Willows Springs and Raleigh. They traveled without bridges over Middle Creek and Swift Creek. The purpose of the trip was to buy Christmas gifts for all the children who attended the Free Will Baptist Church (later to become Mount Pleasant Presbyterian Church) in the Mount Pleasant area. The trip was long with the shopping party arriving back in Willow Springs late in the night but bringing much Christmas joy to the community."

Kelly Lally also noted "Travelers in the mid-nineteenth century still found local transportation impeded by flooded bridges over rivers and muddy creeks often leading to impassable roadways. Fredrick Law Olmsted complained in 1834 he found it better to walk through the woods on either side rather than miring down in the muddy roads."[36]

There were no bridges over the creeks at that time. During the wet season, land travel was almost impossible. Many of the early roads were first wild animal trails, then Indian trails, and finally, Europeans walked along the same trails in search of better farmland.

The Old Covenant Road

William Lipscomb said in an interview in 2017 that "The Old Covenant Road later known as Highway 42 was graded and paved in the winter of 1948/49. The paving project only covered the road beginning at Five Points east to its intersection with highway 50. Beyond highway 50 the road remained unpaved for several more years. When highway 42 was paved, several changes were made to the route. All these changes were made in attempts to straighten the highway. An example of these changes can be seen in the relocation of the road and bridge at Five Points leading to the demise of the community of "Old Shops." One can only assume the other secondary roads around the area remained dirt for many more years." William Lipscomb further said Bud Lipscomb Road (named after his father) was first a dirt path created by roaming cows and pigs connecting Kennebec Road to Old Stage Road around 1910.

Bud Lipscomb Road has had many changes over the years. These changes were also attempts to make the road straight. Each change has resulted in changes to property lines including the present-day Fellowship Baptist Church. Wild animals produced the first trails through this dark corner of Wake County. Early Native Americans used these trails forming trading paths connecting Indian Villages from the mountains to the ocean. These same trails and paths were used by Europeans (mainly English Scotts and Irish) as they pushed westward into Southern Wake County and beyond. These migration patterns brought Europeans and Native Americans in close contact leading to many conflicts.

"In 1774 the French people who occupied Canada and the English who occupied the colonies along the Atlantic seaboard declared a conflict and called it the French and Indian War. The warring parties on both sides made this a prolonged, dreadful, and bloody conflict. The English were finally victorious." However, trust between the English, French, and Native Americans was broken for many future decades. [37]

Just on the heels of the Tuscarora Wars in 1702, John Lawson recounts his travel between his encampment along the Eno River in Durham County to his encampment near Clayton in Johnston County. The route used by Lawson followed along much of what is today Highway 42 through Willow Springs, Myatt's Mill, and Mount Pleasant on his way to an encampment in the Clayton area. "His accounts and travels through North Carolina first published in London in 1709 titled A New Voyage to Carolina are great tools for historical research. By 1741, his second posthumous title, The History of Carolinas, was published and is today one of the most candid, valuable, and readable books of our early history in Wake County. His book has given much detail to the life and times in southern Wake County and beyond. Lawson died in North Carolina at the hands of the Tuscarora Indians."[38] His death led to the Tuscaroran Wars.

The Old Federal Highway

Edith Pearce once said to me in one of our many conversations, "The old Federal highway later known as Old Stage Road has an interesting history to our area. This road continues today as a main travel route for folks commuting to workplaces in Raleigh and beyond. Near the end of the eighteenth century, the federal government developed mail and stage routes. Like much of the road system in Wake County, this road also was often knee deep with sticky mud. Up until the 1960s, a structure existed called the "Old Stage Manor House." It is my assumption this house was built by early members of the Myatt family. This was a stopping place for stagecoaches along the route from Raleigh to Benson. A typical trip to Benson from Raleigh required an overnight at the Willow Springs Stage Manor. Descendants of the Myatt family recall the stage house served meals and spirits to the overnight guest. The spirits were probably wine from the Proctor's vineyard just across the road from the manor house. [39]

Some attempts were made to build a plank road. However, any remnant of these attempts have long since disappeared. About 1910, a trip to Raleigh took several hours one-way crossing many water features along the path. Most of the route was but little more than a dirt trail and no bridges. At times, especially during a wet spring, the roads were impassable. Planned trips to Raleigh were postponed awaiting better conditions. There are accounts by folks walking from Willow Springs to Garner. They said the wagon ruts were so deep and muddy, they walked along the edge of the woods to avoid them.[40]

The Old Tram Road

This road existed until 1948 when work was begun to pave the roads around Willow Spring. The Old Tram Road, now known as Panther Lake Highway, connected the countryside from Old Stage Road at Myatt's Mill Pond (now Panther Lake) and ending at the intersection of Highway 42 at Willow Spring Primitive Baptist Church. The Old Tram Road originally ran behind the farm of Julian Pearce and connected to Willow Spring at Barker's store near the site of the present-day Willow Springs Service Center.[41]

The Old Smithville Road

Old Smithville Road is now highway 1010 and winds along the northern edge of Panther Branch Township beginning at the community of McCullers. The road transverses from west to east through our township heading to Smithfield and east where it crosses highway 70.

William Lipscomb assisted me greatly in understanding our roads. He said that shortly after World War II, the roads around these parts were in great need of paving, widening, and straightening. Much of the work was done between 1946 through 1949 as federal funds were re-appropriated from war time to peace time. The last dirt road to be paved in our area was John Adams Road (circa 2017). That little stretch of John Adams Road was a neat place to stroll on sunny days. I took my children for long walks and talks through there. Like so much of my life, it is the memories that I count, not the money. In the case of this dirt road, it was past time for improvement and I get that; but sometimes those improvements were at the expense of a few good memories. One of the attributes making America such a great place is that our country reinvents itself about every ten years.

The Fayetteville Road

Kelly Lally recalls that "Although no railroads pass through this section of the county, the Fayetteville Road, an early-stage road ran through the township of Panther Branch from north to south beginning in the first decade of the nineteenth century. The store and polling place on Gerard Banks' plantation at the stage road's junction with the "Smithfield Road" became an important stagecoach stop between Raleigh and Fayetteville."[42]

Three Creeks Church

"Thought to have been built around 1880, this simple frame church was the third of four buildings erected for Middle Creek Primitive Baptist Church. The oldest continuing congregation in Wake county, Middle Creek Baptist was first established as "Three Creeks Church" (for nearby Swift, Middle and Black creeks). Today, January 2020, the old church structure is used as a barn along SR 2736."[43]

The Springs at Fuquay

The Springs were located on the farm of a Frenchman named William with the last name Forquet. This Frenchman fought for the Americans and remained in America after the war (1776). After playing with the spelling of the name for a few years, it was finally settled and spelled Fuquay. It just rolls off your tongue better that way. Later, this man bought 1000 acres of land in southwest Wake County. Not long after that purchase his grandson, Stephen, discovered mineral springs (1858) on the property with good water, maybe even having medicinal value. Folks came from far and wide to "take of the waters." Hotels sprang up as well as houses of entertainment. While towns are built by people, springs are constructed by nature and are discovered usually by someone stumbling upon them. With the coming of rail service, thanks to John A. Mills, the little town of Fuquay Springs became a destination. The healing waters were bottled and sold for a short time. By 1920 with the coming of the automobile, trips to the springs became fewer.[44] Elizabeth Reid Murray made the following observation in volume I page 443 of her book "Wake, Capital County of North Carolina" about the springs. She wrote: "Two communities, Holly Springs and Willow Springs, were also named for natural water sources but did not capitalize on any medicinal qualities of their nearby waters."

Today, the Fuquay Springs are still there and with the same healing powers. The only change is that people no longer believe in the magic. Just to give you an idea how strongly folks believed in the healing waters, I read this testimony in the book by K. Todd Johnson and Elizabeth Reid Murray, <u>Wake, Capital County of North Carolina</u>. Page 576, "Troy Honeycutt of Globe Furniture Company in Dunn" reported going to the springs "completely run down" and returned home looking as "fresh and happy as a June Bridegroom."[45] I am not sure what a June bridegroom is supposed to look like, but it sounds good.

When it was found that the soil of the surrounding country was peculiarly adapted to the production of bright-leaf tobacco, farmers from the Granville County area flocked to Fuquay Springs and Willow Spring. Now the people, the tobacco, and the magic are almost gone, but those springs and my memories still linger.

Panther Branch Township

Like so much of my recollection of places and times, this little township cannot be ignored. Most of my story is set in Willow Spring, Myatt's Mill and Varina all in Middle Creek Township. Important to me and this book is that Panther Branch Township is another one of those little gems. "One of Wake County's smallest, Panther Branch was established in 1868. Although no towns have been incorporated in Panther Branch, the township contains a number of distinctive small farming communities that grew up around churches, schools, lodges, gristmills, and stores in the late nineteenth century. These include Cannon Grove, Mount Pleasant, Middle Creek, Gulley's Mill, Turner, Williams Crossroads, Plymouth, Juniper Level, Partin, St. Anna and McCoy; the latter four were primarily African American."[46]

Mrs. Elizabeth Reid Murray in her epic writing of "Wake, Capital County of North Carolina" Volume One observed, "In 1805, the county court gave new and relatively permanent names to the captains' districts. These districts were the forerunners to the modern-day townships. Presently (2021) Wake County has twenty-one townships, with Panther Branch being among the smallest and with no towns included." Just for the record, the exact line for Panther Branch Township starts along the southeast corner of Wake County beginning at Old Stage Road at the point where Harnett County ends and Wake County begins. The line travels northwest to Fannie Brown Road, then left to the west crossing highway 1010 at Holland Church community (Williams Crossroads). The line continues north to the point of Swift Creek crossing. The exact line is hard to follow as part of the line is the Swift Creek as it flows southeast. Willows Spring, the unincorporated community, is actually in the Middle Creek Township but its affrication is in zip code 27592.

For the purposes of this collecting and writing project I have included Willow Spring, Mount Pleasant and Myatt's Mill as if they were all in Panther Branch Township. I do know the difference but it just makes for a better read.

In spite of its lowly status, Panther Branch Township citizens were progressive in their thinking. By 1910, the area boasted of many schools, churches, and lodges. Soon after 1910 came the Corn Clubs, the Canning Clubs, and the Tomato Clubs for the young girls and other rural residents of Panther Branch. "4H" clubs were formed and quickly became a part of the township culture mainly for young boys. The Home Demonstration Clubs, both black and white, were then and are still now, a part of the social and educational fabric of the community."

Early land grants in Southern Wake County, including Panther Branch Township, often provide valuable clues to the people. Lyn Ragan compiled the following information. "This information provides surnames and religious beliefs in and around Wake County about 1675. While documentary evidence of these early settlers of the upper Neuse and Cape Fear Rivers is sketchy it would be logical to assume that after the colony at Jamestown, Virginia was established in 1607 and the rich land proved prosperous, settlement in the Carolinas was inevitable. During the decades 1620-1630 over 20,000 English colonists sailed for Virginia. North Carolina Archives and History (State Library) has available for research an extensive passage list. In 1635 several thousand are listed in that year alone as coming to Virginia and then possibly on to the Carolinas. The very first of these settlers would have claimed land along the major rivers and coast, but as soon as the choice tracts were taken each succeeding wave of colonists pushed out westward to the frontier to stake a claim in the virtually empty wilderness."

Native Americans were not considered as property owners at that time. The bitter civil strife in England in the period 1640-1675 between the king and many Puritans, Quakers, Baptists, Catholics, Episcopalians, and Presbyterians added to the flood of immigrants. When Cromwell beheaded King Charles, many top royalist families fled England including the Washingtons, Jeffersons, Lees, Henrys, Randolphs, and many other families who would play such a leading part in the creation of the new nation.

Since these families were establishing homes one hundred miles from Jamestown by 1660, there is no doubt that they were already arriving on the upper Neuse and Cape Fear at the same time. The granting of the Carolina Charter to the Lords Proprietors in the 1660s was another indication that the new land was ready for settling. Among the passengers listed on the ships in 1635 are many names common to Panther Branch Township a hundred years later when our first surviving census records gave account. For instance, the ship "Constance" sailing on 24 October 1635 lists: William Betts, Robert Session, William Jones, and Henrie Johnson as shipmates, along with many others from the same community near London. The ship "Speedwell" sailing 28 May 1635 lists Richard Rowland, an early name still associated with Willow Spring. All these family names appeared here between the Neuse and Cape Fear with sizeable estates 125 years later. The implication is that these English neighbors stuck together when they staked out their new homes." [47]

"By 1675 King George of England granted 2,800 acres in what is now southern Wake County and more specifically Panther Branch Township to two Myatt brothers. These brothers plowed the virgin soil, raised large crops of cotton, corn and, later, tobacco. The Myatts also raised large families producing many generations of Myatts. By 1903, crop failure in Granville County led many families to relocate to Panther Branch Township in general and Willow Spring in particular. Those folks included the Callis family, the Wilkerson family, and many others. They looked at the soil in Panther Branch Township and moved here. They were the first to grow tobacco commercially. The gold leaf belt was established."

In 1870 the population of Panther Branch Township was 921 souls. By 1910 the population was 1,687 people.[48] By 2010, the communities of Willow Springs, Myatt's Mill, Mount Pleasant, and Panther branch Township had residences from every state in the union and several foreign countries. [49]

Myatt's Mill

"This community in Wake's southern-most corner developed around a grist mill dating to antebellum times and a post office which served the area from 1872 to 1903. Postmasters included William Alford Myatt, E. N. Wilson, James W. Pegram, Edmond H. Wilson, Daniel P, Dove, Benjamin F. Dupree, Alford R. Myatt, David D. Windham and Janius W. Denning. After the Post Office closed, the mail came through Willow Springs. Merchants in the immediate vicinity included general store operators A. J. Blalock, J. W. Adams and W. H. Matthews in the 1880s. Marshall Partin and J. D. Love also operated stores near the mill community. At the beginning of the new century W. A Myatt ran a grist mill, a saw mill, and a cotton gin until his death in 1897. His wife operated the mill until her death in 1910. The mill community had shoemaker, Louis Crouse, two doctors Nathan Blalock and Cornelius Dowd."

Mill ponds were favorite community recreational spots where local residents could swim, fish, and picnic. Myatt's Mill and pond are good examples of this extended use of the property. Several dwellings around the pond were rented as fishing and hunting clubs and some are still standing including the old post office (2021). [50]

The Community of Cardenas

In 1899, one year after the Spanish-American War, a Wake County citizen, Worth Bagley, who died in that conflict while fighting in the town of Cardenas, Cuba, was honored by the naming of this community in his honor. Also named in his honor were a post office, a railroad depot station, a school, and a telephone Company.

Fellowship Presbyterian Church

This church was organized October 26, 1913 and, like her sister church, Willow Springs Presbyterian Church, she too was a mission church of the First Presbyterian Church of Raleigh. This little church held its first meetings in the Harvell/Griffis school located at post station 1749 Bud Lipscomb Road. By 1915, a new structure was completed using the basic blueprint plans of the Granville Presbytery on that site and was debt free. Fellowship Presbyterian Church led a growing band of believers through two world wars, two economic depressions, and a world order turned upside down. This church, located in the southeastern-most corner of Wake County, ran the race and kept the faith until its merger with Willow Springs Presbyterian Church about 1961. Shortly thereafter the two church congregations were united into a new Presbyterian Church called "New Hope." A small group of these men and women from the community near Bud Lipscomb Road chose to remain outside the "New Hope" project and formed the core membership of a new Fellowship Baptist Church. Much of the information contained in this chapter came from some old session records of that first Fellowship Presbyterian Church.

Chapter Six – "The Mighty Multiplying Myatts"

It may seem odd to write an entire chapter about just one family. I do think all families are noteworthy and important. But it is interesting how one family name appears so many times in the church records, social records, the Wake County clerk records, and perhaps other places out here in the land of the Willows. Many early families living around the area of Fellowship Church, first as Presbyterians and later as Baptists, all played a part in flavoring this wonderful area called Willow Springs. It is tempting to try to present a genealogy for all these families. But I must leave that daunting task to the other significant families out here. Each of these families has its own genealogist and their own stories of days gone by. They are knowledgeable and rightfully proud of their family roots, branches, and trees.

There is, however, one big exception to all I have just written. That would be the Myatts. I have looked at their sheer numbers and wondered how they managed to be so plentiful. Here are my general conclusions about these folks. In a search for the earliest wake residents, "first families of the future Wake County", the Myatts are in that elite club.[51]

They came to southern Wake County in two waves: perhaps as early as 1675 with land grants from King George and later with grants in payment for their services to America in our war for independence. Mark Myatt was possibly among the first. He acquired 10 land grants between 1789 and 1796 north and south along Black Creek. Here are a few of their winning combinations that may have led to their prolific numbers. (1) After acquiring land, they stayed close to home for many generations. (2) Where possible, they purchased more land. (3) They had large families with lots of male heirs. You can't turn over a single rock out here without finding a Myatt. All these combinations make them worthy of more study.

No study of Willow Springs or Panther Branch Township can be complete without the Myatt name entering the picture. It is almost un-American to live in this area as I do and not be related to the Myatts—which I am not.

As already noted, the Myatts, no matter how you spell it, were among the earliest residents in this section of Panther Branch Township. The area was named after the Myatts and was known for generations as Myatt's Mill. They were much more than a mill or a pond. They were a community. Elizabeth Reid Murray, in her book, "Wake, Capital County of North Carolina," Volumes I and II, supplied much of this information.

Back in 1979 when I first started collecting and writing The Broken Mirror, Mrs. Murray warned me not to be tempted to let this project turn into a genealogy. Mrs. Murray was an old friend of the Tyndall family and gave me many suggestions and helpful hints on how to collect and write this book. She and my Uncle Forest McLean Tyndall (my Dad's brother) were great friends and were both employed at WPTF Radio in the 1950s. Mrs. Murray was a proofreader for the radio station, while Uncle Forest was an announcer. As it turns out Mrs. Murray was right: genealogy is a slippery slope.

According to Ms. Murray, "W. A Myatt operated a flour and gristmill in the area. Several years before the Civil War, the post office at Myatt's Mill was the center of the community. Just after the Civil War that post office was moved to Willow Springs. Soon afterwards, it was reestablished under the original postmaster. W. A. Myatt. He was appointed postmaster by declaration of the President of the United States. He was followed by postmaster

Peter Dove and many others.

Two brothers of the Myatt family were granted 2,800 acres in southern Wake County. These grants were almost commonplace and date all the way back to Jamestown in 1607. About 1675, King George of England allowed these young men to break the rich, virgin soil with wooden plows. They fertilized the land and raised some of the best cotton ever produced. The real money crop for southern Wake County would be tobacco and appearing much later."[52]

As was the plan for that time, the early grants were first along the North Carolina coast and along the rich bottomland of the three major rivers. As later grants will show, the coastal land grants became scarce and the grants were moved more inland finally arriving in southern Wake County and beyond.

In 1979, Winstead Dove, a descendant of the Myatts, and his family still farmed 22 acres of that original grant in the Willow Springs community. The Doves owned one of the oldest family farms documented in the state and were among several other farm families honored at a home-style barbecue and Brunswick stew dinner. This event was part of the 1979 North Carolina State Fair. Mr. Dove and his family were thanked by Jim Graham, North Carolina Agriculture Commissioner, and Doyle Conner, Agriculture Commissioner from Florida.[53]

Winstead's wife, Betty, is fondly remembered in the area for the wonderful homemade jams, jellies, pickles and craft items she gave to her neighbors on special occasions. Winstead and Betty are buried at a family grave plot on those 22 acres. Winstead Dove stated, "their daughter Cynthia, a high school senior, plans to live at home next year to keep her dogs and horses." The premature death of Cynthia ended those plans. The site of Myatt's mill and post office is now known as Panther Lake. Both the old mill house and post office are still standing (2019).

The name, Panther, is no doubt inspired by the wildlife abounding in the area in earlier times. The area soon had names of the earliest families themselves. Example: Myatt's Branch is still in the same area. The Myatt family was very early associated with southern Wake County, although the earliest of their grants have not survived in the state records. The obituary of Mrs. Mary Myatt, widow of Capt. Mark Myatt, noted that she was "one of the first settlers of this part of the county."[54]

Lord Granville's agents granted John Miate (sic) 500 acres south of the Neuse River on both sides of Swift Creek in 1753. Attached to this grant or "indenture" is a plat describing the land measured for him by surveyor Richard Caswell Jr., three years earlier. Apparently Miate (later spelled Myatt) had built a home or other structures on the site during those three years since the grant mentions his "Improvements." The land was at the time a part of Johnston County.[55]

I know I am devoting a lot of print to the Myatts, but I just cannot shake their connection to my beloved little Willows.

In my final account, I found this story of William Acrill Myatt (born April 22, 1850) in Wake County. "This William was the son of William Alford Myatt and wife Amelia Harrison Myatt. William Alford owned many farms in southern Wake County and a grist mill known as Myatt's Mill. When the post offices came to Panther Branch Township in the 1800s Myatt's Mill had a post office before the civil war, you guessed it, W. A. Myatt was the first postmaster. William Acrill was a descendant of Mark Myatt (possibly his grandson) who was born in England in 1744 and soon moved to Wake County. Mark served in the Revolutionary War as a lieutenant in the cavalry in Captain Soloman Wood's company. He died in 1821. On June 19, 1878 William Acrill married

Columbia Perry. William Acrill and Columbia lived at 121 Blount Street in Raleigh. They had 13 children: Just to keep things real Columbia Perry was related to Joel Lane. Lane sold the land later to be known as Raleigh. That large family brought Myatts to Willow Springs laying a large footprint on the land and the rest of the world in ever increasing numbers."[56]

Kelly A. Lalley, one of Wake County's experts on historical architecture commented, "Members of the Myatt family were among the earliest settlers in Wake County. Mark Myatt settled in the Panther Branch area in the late eighteenth century. It is not known which member of the family built the mill." I would put my money on Mark.

Chapter Seven – My Story and My Family

As for my family's history, let me set up the cast of characters around me. It reads like a Tennessee Williams novel. I was born at Mary Elizabeth Hospital in Raleigh, North Carolina on January 19, 1941. Robert E. Lee, Dolly Parton, and I all share that same birth date albeit different years. After a brief stay at the hospital, Mom and I returned to our little apartment over Thomas Drug Store on Broad Street in Varina.

I was small in frame for my age. Only four words come to my mind when describing myself: "boundless energy" and "inexhaustible curiosity." My neighbors called me "Flash." I lived by a simple rule: "why walk when you can run," and run I did. Fast like the wind. I wanted to see what was under every rock and why it was there. I had endless questions for everyone. My small frame and big black eyes got me another nickname "polka dot." This name stayed with me for much of my young life.

Marvin Thomas, my brother was eighteen months older than me. He was the smart student and everyone liked him. He grew to be tall with a light complexion and wore glasses from an early age. He was a great dancer with many girlfriends. Just out of high school, he bought a 1959 Plymouth Fury complete with the tail fins. That sure was a pretty car. Once he let me borrow it, and I tossed a cigarette out the window. It whipped around, reentered through a back window, and burned a hole in the backseat. He was not happy with that little event and never let me borrow his car again. In high school, he was quiet and never got into trouble. My story was a little different.

Our apartment over Thomas Drug store consisted of three rooms, a shared hallway, and a shared bathroom. The shared bathroom was with other upstairs families. That is where life began for me with a mother, a dad, and an older brother, Marvin Thomas, whom we called Tom.

Tom recalled that Louise and Nelson Meadows had space up there as well as Miss Leora Tally. As he further recalled, Miss Tally was an unwed lady from Apex and occupied the front rooms along Broad Street. These rooms were most desired as they looked out over downtown Varina. Miss Tally spent many happy hours just sitting and rocking while looking out over a sleepy Varina. It must have been a great sight back then. Tom could not recall why or when Miss Tally arrived in Varina. I was too young to remember any of this. These accounts are the recollections of my brother.

Our stay over Thomas's Drug store was brief. War with Germany and Japan was declared on December 7, 1941. Very soon our little family moved to Newport News, Virginia. The year was 1942 and the war in Europe and the Pacific was raging. My Dad, William Thomas Tyndall, took a job in the naval shipyards in nearby Norfolk. He received a military deferment because he had two sons and a wife. Dad also had four brothers serving in America's armed forces in both theaters of war. We lived in a subdivision built by the United States Defense Department just for families working in the Navy shipyards. It was called Copeland Park. My Dad was not a "draft dodger" and wanted to do his part. Many young fathers in this time period 1941-1945 volunteered for this type of employment instead of the military draft into active army service. There he worked long hours with little pay during many dark days of World War II. My mother also worked in a nearby Norfolk defense factory. I recall her stories of how she drove a tractor delivering airplane parts around the military bases.

Times were bleak, but at least the family was all together. My brother Tom and I had no idea what was going on in a world of war and turmoil. Tom insists he remembers the programmed "blackouts" during World War ll when folks living near the coast in both Virginia and North Carolina would listen for the sirens to sound and all the lights were shut off. Black window shades were pulled down and the light in our little house was dimmed. This was done both in businesses and in private homes. The purpose was to make the night as dark as possible to prevent or hamper enemy air raids. The war was not thousands of miles from us. There are accounts of the night skies lighting up when German submarines sank our merchant ships just off the coasts of North Carolina and Virginia.

After the war ended in 1945, our little family moved back to Varina. We lived in several locations. At first, we lived at 707 East Broad Street in a rented house right across the street from an old cotton gin. That old gin was a great place to play and explore. Later, for a short time, we lived in a house on Durham Street that we shared with another family. Their names were Lura and Andrew Maynard. While living there, our kerosene cook stove caught fire one night. We all got out safely, but to this day I still remember the smell of burning kerosene.

At the Durham Street address, we had a man living in our garage. His name was Purvis Wood. Now that may sound a little strange, but I am told it was not uncommon to have guests in other parts of the home. Everyone could not afford housing in the late 1940s. Mr. Wood was a gentle old soul and told me many stories. I am sorry I do not know what happened to him. We moved around a lot in those early years after returning from Norfolk. We finally settled in a rented, shotgun style house at 605 North Street, one block from my Broad Street playground. Our house was rented from Mrs. Annie Adams Akins on the hill who I referred to earlier.

Dad had many short-lived jobs during this time. About 1950, he took a job as a night watchman in Varina. Home ownership was out of the question for us. Dad spent a lot of time away from the family. I am not sure why. As of 2015, the North Street house was still standing and filled with my memories. Those memories are tucked away in my mind. Only I can re-erect them as I do every time I ride down North Street.

When we lived there, we were two houses up from the Gold Leaf Warehouse. The warehouse has since been removed in the name of progress in 2018. Before the warehouse was built, the land was a cow pasture for the Akins family. They had a lot of farm animals around their house. That pasture was also a great playground for me, as was the warehouse. As a child the house seemed so much larger than it is today. I guess things look bigger when you are five years old nurturing an urge to explore and question everything.

With all my bottomless energy and curiosity, I had many jobs, or as I called them, ventures at an early age. I worked at the Varina Theater selling popcorn. Nessie Oliver sold tickets. Mr. Wade owned the theater. Alford and Doris Stephenson managed the theater. The pay was not much, but I got free popcorn. Yes, Varina had its own theater and so did Fuquay Springs. I was about 9 or 10 years old and supplemented my theater job with a paper route delivering "The Raleigh Times" to 30 customers in Varina. To this day, I remember most of my customers. Each day after delivering the newspaper to them, I had a conversation with them. Mrs. John Brown showed me how to milk a cow—a skill I never quite perfected. Mrs. Brown and I had many conversations. She seemed to be a very wise lady.

I was about ten years old when I started selling clothes hangers to the local dry cleaners for a penny apiece. I also sold soda drink bottles to the local grocery stores for one cent each. I sold fishing worms and "get well soon" cards to my neighbors. Roy Wilson was my best fishing worm customer. I dug the worms from my secret place behind the Gold Leaf Warehouse. Viola Wood was my best card customer. Not only did she pay me for the cards, she gave tips and sometimes a slice of her famous yellow cake with royal white icing. Viola was such a sweet lady. We talked often about the way things were for her when she was my age. Viola and husband, Coy Wood, shared a house with Pat and Aleen Gray. The Grays had two sons, Donald and William. We played together often. One day, while the Gold Leaf warehouse was being built, we pushed their outhouse (toilet) over the hill. It seemed like a good idea at the time. The Grays also had a daughter, Bonnie Jean, who was older than me.

When I was fifteen, I worked at Poe's Red and White in Varina. At about age nine, I made my first dollar by selling one gallon of blackberries to Mrs. Stella Eakes. Mrs. Eakes had a beauty shop behind Thomas' Drug store in Varina. It was not my first dollar ever, but it was the first sale when I was paid with a real one-dollar bill. I was so proud of that dollar. While still in college, I worked summers at Cornell Dublier Electrics plant in Fuquay Springs. I also worked for Lena Mangum at the Spring View Grill (now closed and eight miles South of Fuquay-Varina). Lena was a great friend. She helped me in many ways. I remember one Christmas she gave me a new London Fog jacket and my first bleeding madras shirt. Many times, she gave me extra money for my work. It sure did come in handy during those lean college years. Her husband Marvin was a disabled veteran. Many Sunday afternoons, she and I would visit him at the Veterans Hospital in Cumberland County.

When I was eleven years old, I worked at Cooper's Grocery store in Fuquay Springs as a bag boy. I got paid $7.29 in a small brown paper bag for sixteen hours work which included Friday afternoons and fourteen hours on Saturdays. The other bag boys and I were not allowed to sit down. It was one of the Cooper rules. Even then, I thought $7.29 was cheap labor. I guess the child labor laws did not apply to poor children. I was willing to work for whatever Mr. Hobson Cooper was willing to pay.

Cooper's Grocery was located between a card shop and Ashworth's Clothing Store, both along Main Street in downtown Fuquay Springs. Both Mrs. Ashworth and Mrs. Morton Ransdell (Ransdell Shoe Store) were kind to me. They both had Saturday night snacks at their stores and shared them with me. Every summer I worked in tobacco for several local farmers. Even back then, I bought groceries for the family from my meager earnings I always tried to save money. I had my own bank account at the Bank of Varina at a very young age. Somehow, I knew saving money was more fun than spending it. Today at age seventy-nine, I still feel that way. Another thing I learned at a young age was that the key to "breaking the rent cycle" was becoming educated, so I was intent on getting an education.

I greatly appreciate my humble beginnings on North Street. I learned so much and was not even aware of it. When I look back at the folks around me when I was growing up, I am reminded that they are a part of who I am today, and I want to say to them "thank you"—albeit a little late. My childhood had its share of pain but also large shares of joy and pride.

I cannot say the Tyndall family played any major part in shaping the flavor of southern Wake County. My father and his family did move to Willow Springs about 1930 after losing their family farm as a result of the agriculture depression in Greene County. They went from land owning farmers to tenant farmers in a short period of time.

My grandmother, Kathleen Susan Tyndall, became the first PTA president at Willow Spring Elementary School (circa 1933). I do recall Kathleen Tyndall having four stars in her window denoting that she had four sons all serving their country during World War II. They all returned from the war safely. Kathleen had a stroke in 1950 leaving her paralyzed and speechless for the remainder of her life. The few visits we made to see her were in a rest home somewhere near South Raleigh. Her room was on the second floor of a converted brick house. I recall the property was a dairy with lots of barns out back—perfect for exploration. She could not speak but made growling sounds. We were required to sit in her lap and kiss her goodbye. I was terrified to do that. I am sorry to report that I knew very little about my Grandmother Tyndall but have been told that in her younger days she was quite outspoken for her time.

Grandmother Tyndall had a younger half-sister named Louise. She married Gilmore Spivey from Willow Springs. Later, she got a degree in nursing from Watts Hospital in Durham and became the county nurse for Carteret County. Even though she was a Great Aunt to me, I was very close to her and was very impressed with her. During the Roosevelt years of Franklin and Eleanor, Aunt Louise was great friends with them. Aunt Louise was a big supporter of Eleanor in her many efforts to lift everyone out of the darkness and hopelessness of poverty and into the sunshine of hope for a better tomorrow. Franklin Roosevelt once said, "All we have to fear is fear itself." To this day I do not understand what that meant. Our family has pictures, letters and news articles involving Aunt Louise. Aunt Louise also wrote a weekly news column for the Carteret County newspaper over the years.

Lizzie Mae Honeycutt Tyndall, my mother, developed Tuberculosis in the mid-1940s and was sent away to a sanatorium for treatment by order of the Wake County Health Department and enforced by the Wake County Sheriff Department According to an account by Roy G. Taylor, "Tuberculosis scared us to death. It was a death sentence. The people with TB would start falling off so fast they became a mere shell of themselves in only a few months. The public shied away from the folks with TB as if it were the plague. The few caregivers would not get close to the victims. People were afraid to breathe the same air as the victim. When death finally came the bed sheets and clothing were burned. Folks ran from the flames in mortal fear." [57]

My mother was a beautiful young woman. To me she was always the "belle of the ball." Her jet-black hair, pleasant smile, and happy laugh endeared her to many folks. She always had lots of friends around our house. They played "Rook" and "Set Back"; they laughed and joked until the wee hours of the morning. Interestingly, all these things with Mom took place after her return from the sanatorium. She was a survivor.

Mom never learned to cook. Louise, our next-door neighbor, would cook wonderful cakes and Mom would quietly slide them onto her cake plate and serve them with that warm smile and a wink of her dark brown eyes. She never did tell us the whole truth about who baked the cakes. Later, after Dad died, she finally learned and was an excellent cook.

My brother Tom recalled Mother left us for the sanatorium on a Wednesday, three days before Christmas 1947. She had no choice as the county health department ordered her into quarantine at the Wake County Tuberculosis Sanatorium in North Raleigh (Whitaker Mill Road). That building is still standing today (2021) and is known as May View Assisted Living Center. It must have been a sad time for all, but, to tell you the truth, I do not remember much of it. My knowledge of these early events came to me from Tom and my mother's younger sister, Mary Gladys Stokes. Aunt Mary also had tuberculosis and was in a sanatorium in the Blue Ridge Mountains of Virginia. Aunt Mary told me many stories of my earlier childhood. My parents, for whatever the reason, just did not talk about things like that.

Mother's Tuberculosis coupled with my Dad's frequent absences were major events in my early life. It removed a mother, and most of the time, the father from the family setting. Things changed quickly for us. My Dad did his best, but he was not able to keep his family together. My brother and I were moved around to relatives quite a bit in those first days, weeks, and months after Mother left. I do remember some of this time. As I recall, my aunts and uncles were discussing what to do with us. Some of the solutions were not too pleasant. My brother remembers talk of an orphanage.

Just in the nick of time as the orphanage door was about to become a reality, Tom and I settled in with my grandmother, Mrs. Gertrude Foster Honeycutt at our North Street house. We called her Miss Gerty. I did not remember her before she came to live with us. As was the rule in those times, when the aging parent could no longer maintain a household, they gave up their own home and moved around from child to child. This was the case with Miss Gerty. She had given up housekeeping and was living with my uncle Douglas on one of the Judd farms near Fuquay Springs. She did not want to take on a new family, but, under the circumstances, her choices were as limited as ours. I do recall she was not well at that time but said very little about her illnesses. She never complained but most always had a sad expression. I can't remember her saying much. She probably did not look forward to raising two more boys. Finally and reluctantly, she would come to live with us. Dad agreed to pay the monthly rent and not much else. She would look after the house and us.

Dad would come by for visits from time to time. Miss Gerty had one primary rule for me. No doubt I needed it: "you have to mind me or off you go." That stern warning stuck with me for a long time. When Miss Gerty moved in with us, she brought many new and strict rules like no porch furniture was allowed. Her logic for this rule was if you do not have a job, don't sit on the front porch and let everyone know you are unemployed. Always close the door when leaving the room even in summer and always cut off the light. Our little house had a living room but we never used it. Miss Gerty kept plastic covers over all the furniture. That always baffled me. Miss Gerty said she was saving that room for Mother's return.

Miss Gerty did smile at me when I got into trouble "which was often." She would let me sit in her lap and tell me I needed to do better and then came a big kiss scented with snuff. To deal with all the events around my life, I would often laugh and make jokes about all the mess around us.

I was quite a talker. I think it was a way to gain attention and perhaps convince someone to think of me as special. Inside, I was sad because we were so poor. Things were not good with us financially. I did not know all the stuff kids know these days. But I could tell things were greatly out of order. I was ashamed of our financial plight. I did not know just how poor we were until one day the Wake County Welfare Department came and told us.

Miss Gerty, who saved me from the orphanage, was a small frail woman with gray hair always arranged in a tight gray ball at the back of her neck. She dipped snuff, so she needed a spit can nearby at all times. She looked frail and her soft gray eyes were sad. She spoke very little but did provide us with meals. In the winter we had beans: first white, then brown, and then red. On the fourth day, the color scheme would start all over again. Most often the beans were served with potatoes. I remember saying to myself, "not potatoes again." I never said it out loud. Meat was a special treat. If the meat was pork chops, we got one piece per person, and the same was true for chicken. We rarely ate meals together. To this day, I do not understand why we did it that way. I ate my beans when I got hungry and was grateful for them. We heated only one room in the winter. After the beans were cooked on our kerosene stove in a cold kitchen, Miss Gerty would move the big pot to the oil heater in her bedroom. That is where she sat and rocked long hours. She may have been dreaming of times gone by, of better times, or not dreaming at all. It is true the menu was limited, but we never went hungry.

On rare occasions she made a dessert she called a two-egg pudding. It was simply a one-layer cake with no icing. She wrapped the cake in a towel and stored it in her pie safe. Boy, was it good! To this day when I sometimes open her old pie safe which I have at my house now, I still get a quick faint smell of that two-egg pudding even after all these years. I guess memories come to us as smells just as well as stories.

While I tried not to let my friends know about my mother and her tuberculosis, the word soon got out in the neighborhood and school. Folks did not know then what they know now. Tom and I were bullied at school by remarks made by our class mates. I remember one such occasion when a "so called friend" said he could not play with me anymore. His mother said he could die if he touched me. That remark hurt to the core. I did not know what to say. I recall with great clarity the many episodes of bullying. The person being bullied had no defense. If I fought back, I would risk making the conflict more intense or getting punished.

I did fight back once while on the playground at Fuquay Springs Elementary school. I lost that fight, and it was me who got in trouble for starting it. Fighting on the playground was strictly forbidden. To this day, I remember the persons who were doing the bullying. I will spare them the embarrassment and hurt they caused by not sharing their names here. They probably do not recall the incidents, but I sure do. I choose to forgive and take the high ground. Forgiving is not hard to do but the forgetting takes time and wisdom.

Tom and I were screened every 90 days by the Wake County Nurse to be sure we did not show signs of tuberculosis. The screening required three needle pricks in the right arm. If the pricks turned red further testing was required. I watched my arm carefully in mortal fear I would have signs of TB and be sent away. Thank God that never happened. We received regular county assistance from the Welfare Department during those years. I remember the long boxes of processed cheese, the gray cans of mystery meat, powdered milk and eggs, the used clothes, the free school lunch tokens, and the used toys. One of my greatest desires was to have toys, clothes, and shoes that had a new smell to them. Instead, I had recycled clothes that smelled aged and musty.

Who could forget those big brown government vans as they drove up to our little house? The vans looked like our present-day UPS trucks. I think about that every time I see one. The welfare ladies always wore brown uniform dresses. They were always proper but spoke shortly to us. They looked serious and talked to us in deep stern voices. I believed they had eyes to see right through me, so I was afraid of them. My brother once told me he was going to put me in the back of one of those vans, and I would never be heard or seen again. Now that I am an adult and starting to collect and write my memories, I realize those welfare ladies were kind, loving people providing a needed service. I have come to understand if it were not for that safety net they provided, my story might have had a different ending. That is just the way you see things when you are six years old and unsure about yourself or your tomorrow.

Our little family was dysfunctional to say the least. Before my dad passed in 1967, I forgave him for all the absences from our family. Forgiving and forgetting are not always the same event and often do not occur at the same time. Both require time, the great healer of all things.

William Thomas Tyndall, my dad, did not finish high school and that led to many short-lived and dead-end jobs for him. I remember one of his jobs was driving a drycleaning truck. He had very little to say to me growing up, but he always made time to chat with other folks. He was well-liked on North Street and Varina. He played the banjo quite well or so I am told. I never recall him playing for me.

Dad was hired as a night watchman for the community of Varina around 1950. Tom told me lots of stories before his own passing in August 2017. He said Mother and Dad were considering separation but the TB changed that. He said Dad and I never got along, and he did not know the reason. I guess some things are just better not known.

I have several cousins on the Tyndall side. Many of them have told me similar stories about their dads. Cousin Jim Tyndall and I talk often. He lives in Northern Virginia. Recently he told me that our dads wanted to be good parents but did not know how. He may be right about that. I grew up thinking I was the problem and perhaps I was; but Jim's answer makes good sense now. Many of the arguments Dad and I had over the years stemmed from my firm commitment to go to college. This was my dream even at an early age. Dad just could not understand why I was dead set on "getting above my raising." I insisted that was exactly why I wanted to get more education. We both got a little loud while making our points. I regret losing respect for a parent and later asked his forgiveness.

Someone once wrote, "the first to apologize is the bravest; the first to forgive is the strongest; and the first to forget is the happiest." Time is the great healer of all things.[58]

My father firmly believed I should be content working at Cornell Dubilier, the first manufacturing plant to come to Fuquay Springs. He said if I worked hard, I might even get to be a line supervisor one day. Being a Cornell employee was never in my plan. That plant did a lot of good for the economy in southern Wake County, but, in my view, it never did much to help folks get ahead. The employees lived in mortal fear—fear of the Labor Union coming and Cornell firing everyone who ever spoke the word or dared think of organizing. I remember from my summer jobs at Cornell how the employees worked hard to meet production expectations only to find the level raised higher almost daily.

Dad and I had our last conversations (arguments) on the matter of a college education when Dad made it clear, he would not pay one red cent to help me with the college expenses. I was not asking for any help. I just wanted his affirmation for that endeavor. He said it was a foolish, big dream of a foolish, little boy. Mother heard most of these conversations but never said a word in my defense. I think she was afraid of him even in his disabled condition.

I attended Campbell College from 1960 to 1964. Four years later, I graduated with honors, making the Dean's list and earning a Bachelor of Science Degree in Business Administration. I paid for all of it—every red cent! I am sorry Dad and I never agreed on this matter and saddened by his refusal to go to my high school or college graduations. He even skipped my wedding. But I am not sorry I did all those things.

This dysfunctional little family had yet another character: my uncle, Mother's brother, Clifton Honeycutt. We called him Uncle Tank. He lived with us part of the time while on disability from WWII. This resulted in many emotional and psychological problems for him in later life. Back then we called it "shell shock;" today, it is called "post traumatic syndrome." One day, he left for cigarettes at the nearby service station and did not come back for several years. On another of those long unexplained absences, we received word his body had been recovered from the Biloxi Bay in Mississippi. My two aunts in Richmond got the money together to have his body returned to us. He had a military funeral and was buried at the Military cemetery in Raleigh. I have his flag.

Miss Gerty would not allow pets to live in the house. That did not stop me. I converted our old shed out back into my own zoo. Coy Wood and his sweet wife Viola who lived down the street from us raised and sold parakeets. From time to time some birds were hatched with genetic defects, like only one wing or one foot. They gave me all the culls. I named them all Pete or Repete. I also kept white mice. I ordered them from a matchbook cover advertisement. It did not take long before I had too many white mice and had to turn them all loose. I have been told that even today in Varina along North Street folks see white rats running around, possibly descendants of my horde.

Margaret Hall, the Varina Post Office Mistress, liked me and let me bid on live chicks shipped by mail. If folks who ordered the chicks failed to pick them up or failed to pay the postage, the chicks were auctioned off. Mrs. Hall made sure I was the only one bidding. The boxes, filled with living and dead chicks, were sold to the highest bidder. The proceeds from the sale were used to pay the expense of shipment. I did not pay much for a box of chicks as most had not survived the journey. My business plan was to raise and sell the chickens. Somehow that did not work out. I could not part with the lucky ones that lived. My collection continued to grow until a hungry dog got in the shed and killed most of them.

As for cats, I lost count of the number. They were all named Tinker Bell, followed by a number. My best friend was "Rusty," my dog. I talked to him, and I am convinced he understood what I was saying. He was a mix of a German Shepherd and other parts unknown, but I was told he came from a good neighborhood. Rusty and I were always side-by-side. We would race up and down the sidewalks of Varina. I won most of those races. Rusty lived a long time. One day he just up and left. I am sure he died peacefully, but I was sorry to have been deserted by my longtime friend.

The rent on our house was paid each month on the last Saturday of the month between 12 noon and 4pm to Miss Annie Akins. As I recall, Mrs. Akins would sit in the back of Kannan's Clothing Store, pocketbook wide open waiting for the rent money. There she visited with Anisa. We called her Alice and her husband (Kahlil) was just called "K." They were a delightful couple, first generation folks from Syria. Miss Annie was not mean to me but was a stern no-nonsense business woman. She only wanted the rent money. The conversation and smiles were rare—at least with me. Miss Gerty always worried about getting the rent in on time. I was the one charged with the responsibility of taking the rent to Mrs. Akins. To this day I still remember carrying that money to town and facing Miss Annie. I was so very proud to be the one to take on that responsibility.

We lived in that rented house on North Street from 1945 until 1967. As I recall, we never asked for any repairs on our house for fear the rent would increase accordingly. After Mother's return from the sanatorium, she and Miss Annie became great friends and visited often with each other. An African American woman named Mabel who worked for Miss Annie was also another friend to Mother. Now that I am a little older, perhaps my recollection of events is not accurate, but that is how I recall those times.

In the early summer just after school was out, many of the local churches had Bible School that usually lasted a week. To allow kids the chance to attend more than one Bible School, the sessions were at different times. By then I had my new Donald Duck bicycle. I won it by entering a Dr. Pepper contest and collecting the most bottle caps. That was another one of those days I would describe as among the best days of my life. Not only did I own a new bicycle, but it also smelled new. All the boys from North Street would attend Bible School but only in time for the refreshments. My family did not go to a church then, so I went to all the Bible Schools. My choice of denomination was not based on any sound religious doctrine but who had the best refreshments. Wake Chapel Christian Church won hands down with a whole bottled drink just for me and a candy bar every day. Fuquay Baptist came in a distant last with only one small cup of watered-down juice and one small cookie.

The little boys from North Street were a force to be reckoned with, all of us riding our bicycles to Bible School. We tried to look tough. I pinned a playing card (ace of spades) on the front rim of my bike using a clothespin. As I rode along, it sounded like a motorcycle. Those were great times for me. I was the leader of the pack. The North Street gang usually included Tom, Eddie Ragan, and David and Edgar Stephenson. The group dynamics changed from time to time but we were the core.

Life on North Street moved on at a slow pace. I knew everyone on our street and visited with every one of them almost daily. At Christmas, we did not have many decorations, but we got to see and enjoy our neighbors' displays every night. Mrs. Nelson Meadows (we called her Louise) had lovely Christmas lights, and when she turned them on each night they would bubble. Those were the most beautiful things I had ever seen.

After nearly a five-year absence from my life my mother, Lizzie Mae, returned. Just before she came home, I remember everyone saying to me "I'll bet you are looking forward to having your mother back home." I was, but I was not sure where or how she was going to fit back into my life. Five years was a long time, almost half my life at that time. I had gotten along just fine without a mother and was not sure how we would reconnect. The day she returned, she brought gifts for us all. She gave me a fingernail brush cleaner. I didn't know what it was. She said we had to boil it first to be sure there were no germs on it. That scared me so badly, I never used it. Mother had to take her meals separate from the rest of us. She even had dinner plates and cups washed separately from us. They were bright blue in color. Miss Gerty told me not to touch mother's plates as it could kill me. One day when no one was looking, I touched the plate, the cup, and all the silverware several times in sheer defiance.

Not everything was bad for me. Mother and I got off to a slow start, but we did connect, and I learned to love her all over again. I cared for her until her death in 1994. She never talked much about her time away from us. I guess we did not know the right questions to ask.

When I was 14, my Dad suffered a brain hemorrhage and died ten years later. When he returned from a long stay at Rex Hospital in Raleigh, he could not speak or move his legs. He cried a lot. After a few months, Willard Council, the Fuquay Springs town manager, came to our North Street house to collect Dad's things that belonged to the town. He said there would be no more paychecks. Dad had only recently taken a job as a full-time police officer/night watchman with the town of Fuquay Springs. He opted out of the Social Security program in favor of the retirement system for law enforcement officers. That was a bad choice for him to make as it resulted with our family having no income. Roy Wilson and Nelson Meadows built my dad a swinging bar suspended from the ceiling of the front bedroom over his hospital bed. With it, he learned to turn himself over in the bed. Those were some hard times for us all. Mother never complained and looked after him for all those years. When he died in 1967 Mother never cried. I asked why. Her answer was classic; "I have no more tears left, son."

In 1959, I made application and was accepted at Campbell College for the school year beginning in 1960. I never told Mother or Dad I was going to do this. I knew there was no need. Somehow, I managed with all my many jobs to put together the money. In 1960, I entered Campbell College (now Campbell University) and four years later I graduated, making the Dean's list with a Bachelor of Science degree in Business Administration and no college loan debt. To this day, I do not know how I did that. I was the first of my generation (the Tyndalls and the Honeycutts) to go to college and graduate. I share this not to brag but to reveal a little of my determination to break the poverty and rent cycle for myself and later my own little family. In life, if the tough things do not kill you, they will make you stronger.

I married Judith Godwin (July 6, 1963) the love of my life since ninth grade. By 1964, I graduated from College. That same year, I got a job in State Government, first at the Department of Transportation and later at the Department of Insurance.

Chapter Eight – Special People of North Street

I guess Hillary Clinton was right when she wrote, "It Takes a Village" to raise a child. That was exactly the way it was done on North Street. There were approximately ten families living along North Street and the surrounding blocks. With a few exceptions, they were a part of my life for a long time. Very few families moved to North Street and even fewer left. The adults in these families looked after all of us young folks. When they saw we were up to no good, they scolded us with stern looks and sharp words. We listened to them and obeyed just as if they were our parents. Truly, they were more than neighbors. They were like my extended family. They were such a big part of my younger days in Varina that it would be unthinkable to leave them out. This is not a complete list. If I have omitted someone, please charge it to my head and not to my heart.

Louise and Nelson Meadows who lived beside us were great friends. They were like parents to me. Louise always had Cokes at her house and was willing to share with me. Nelson always said a "cold Coke and a BC powder first thing each morning gets your day off to a good start." Nelson took all the kids on the block down to Mr. Joe Stephenson's pond for afternoon swims. He would drive his green oil delivery truck along the dam of the pond, and we would all just jump off and into the deep end of the pond. If you could not swim, you learned fast. Nelson also had a pet monkey named Charlie. He kept Charlie in a small cage in his backyard. Once Charlie got loose, and it took us all day to get him back in his cage. Just a word of warning: Monkeys never make good pets. They are fast runners and inclined to bite. Rusty and I sure did have fun chasing ole Charlie.

Louise and Nelson took me to Carolina Beach for my first look at the ocean. That trip also ranks among the best days of my life. We rode down to the beach in Nelson's green oil truck. He delivered heating oil in the winter months to the locals and fuel oil in the summer months to all the tobacco farmers during curing season. I will never forget the Meadows and their kindness. On rare occasions everyone on North Street got together and cooked chickens on a cot frame over a pit of hot coals in the ground. This was done in Louise and Nelson's backyard. The BBQ chickens were just good. The thing that stuck in my mind was that on those special days I could drink as many soft drinks as I wanted. My best record was seven.

Louise's mother, **Mrs. Ella Overby**, lived with Louise and Nelson most of the time and was so kind to me. Her conversations of days gone by in downtown Angier and her wise advice will always be remembered. I still remember the smell of her yeast rolls. They were good and she shared them with everyone on North Street. Almost every Christmas, Mrs. Overby baked a fruit cake for her family. It was the biggest thing I ever saw. She kept it in a wash tub covered in a white pillow case soaked in wine. This made her cold, back porch smell like a winery.

When Judy and I got married on July 6, 1963, Mrs. Overby gave us an old oak chest. She said "I have no money or gifts to give you but you might like to have the chest to remember me by." I still hold dear that chest and the memories of her kindness. Great treasures are not always gold or silver. Sometimes they can be made of oak.

Milking the cows with Beatrice Brown:

When I was just a young lad, Mrs. John Brown (Beatrice) was on my route and we often talked about her good ole days. Once while milking her cow named Bessie, she said "Son, you have to be gentle with cows. Just like people they don't like being rushed. There are a few rules you must follow. Always wash your hands with warm water. That helps to relax the cow. Nobody likes cold hands on a cold morning. Next rule is to talk to your cow. It does not matter what you talk about. They especially like politics and religion." She then said "Son, do you know what is worse than the cow kicking over the milking pail halfway through the milking process? I said no. She said, "The cow kicking it when the pail is full." We both had a good laugh. She continued to smile and milk. I continued to ask questions. I do not recall what the cow said.

Mrs. Brown told me that she and her husband John moved to the little village of Varina where John was to become the railroad agent. A little depot was built and named Varina Station. When they got there, she could walk to the depot and the small shopping area. The road later was called Broad Street. Back then it was dirt with trees lining the walkways.

They had a big garden, chickens, ducks, and, of course, ole Bessie. The ducks were good for the garden; they ate the bugs and not the plants. I remember making notes after her conversations. Over the years I lost the notes but not the memories of Mrs. Brown and Bessie. She let me try to milk Bessie once but that did not go well. At least Bessie didn't kick over my pail.

Merd and Vaughn Phillips: They lived across the street from us in Varina. Mrs. Phillips took a lot of time with me in those early days. I remember her telling me stories of her childhood. She could tell a ghost story to rival the best storytellers in the world. I included one of her classic best stories in my section entitled "Murders, Mysteries." She once said to me:

> *"Son, you are only poor if you choose to be that way."*

I did not understand then but I think I know now what she was talking about. She also said:

> *"Do not let others fill your cup for you. They will put into it what they want you to have. If you fill your cup yourself you can choose what and how much you put in it."*

How wise this great lady was to have known that. How kind of her to take the time to tell me even if I didn't fully understand. Most summer afternoons she sat on her large front porch rocking. I went over there almost every day. Mrs. Phillips dipped snuff and she could spit five feet. Her aim was so accurate, she could knock flies off her potted plants and never get a drop of snuff on the porch.

Jo Ann and R. L. lived across the street from us, too. R. L. was the son of Vaughn and Merd. I don't remember much about them. They were younger than my parents. R. L. did work for the railroad as did Merd. Jo Ann was sister to Maggie Holland. She married R. L. and moved to North Street just out of high school. She was then, and still is, a very pretty lady. Very shortly after our return from Norfolk. Flossie Phillips Powell and her daughter Peggy came to live with Merd and Vaughn, Flossie's parents. It really is a small world. Flossie and Peggy were our neighbors in Copeland Park, Virginia and just a few years later they were our neighbors again on North Street. I have great memories of them. Peggy was a little older than me and I often thought of her as my big sister. She had all the records from the fifties, which we played over and over dancing the nights away. Merd and Vaughn just sat watching us while smiling and clapping time to the music.

Pearl and Herman Tutor: They were also across the street. Later, they built a house and opened Tutor's Grocery on the west end of Broad Street in Varina. The Tutors were kind to me but Pearl was always ready to give me unsolicited advice. They did not appreciate it when I would walk or run across their grass. They said I was wearing a path through the yard. I am not sure how I could do that. I continued to walk through the yard only when they were not looking. I never did see a path.

Alice Bullock:

I surely do remember her. She and her daughter Shena ran a grocery store (Bullock's Meat Market) located on downtown Broad Street. Once, I let the live chickens that Mrs. Bullock kept in the back of the store get out of their cages. Miss Gerty found out about my misadventure. She made me go back to the store and tell Mrs. Bullock what I had done and that I was sorry. Mrs. Bullock said she accepted my apology and helped me round up the chickens. I was happy she accepted my apology but still sad for the poor caged chickens. Those chickens could be free today if only they had run a little faster. Did I tell you I was the fastest runner in all of Varina at that time? On that day I ran as slow as I could to help the chickens be free.

Fred and Leora Ragan:

The Ragans lived up the street from the Tyndalls. They took me to Pullen Park to swim in a real pool with a cement bottom and two diving boards. They would always let me swim until the pool closed to gather us up for the ride back to Varina. We were all in one car: the Ragans, their son Eddie, Jimmy Meadows, Edgar Stephenson, my brother Tom, and myself. I am still not sure how we all could fit into that car but, somehow, we did. Thinking back over their kindness, taking all the neighborhood kids to Pullen Park was a large undertaking. I never heard them say a harsh word to me or anyone else. As I recall, both of them worked for Parker's Furniture store. They were the first people I ever knew who moved off North street, breaking the rent cycle, and into a brick house they bought. Mrs. Ragan was afraid she would never be able to make the mortgage payments but she did and paid the house off several years early.

Odell Smith:

She could make the best fudge ever and allowed me to lick the pot clean every time. Her husband Wade was a man of few words but never asked us to go home. Odell was the best Rook player I ever knew. She was the social director of the street. She arranged all those BBQ chicken suppers. She was also the most caring and giving person I ever knew. She was among my mother's best friends. Odell had a way about her that made everyone feel better. She smoked cigarettes, and, in the end, it was the cigarettes that finally got the best of her. She had one son, Ralph, who preceded her in death. She had a hard time dealing with that, but never lost her zest for life.

Katherine Johnson Tutor:

I interviewed her about some of her days now gone by. We had a nice sit-down talk on May 1, 2018, and I recorded much of it. Kitty, as we knew her, grew up along the western edge of Apex in Wake County. She attended high school in Apex where she played high school basketball. It was at one of those basketball games that she first met her future husband, Paul. Kitty said she knew he was the one. But in all fairness, she had to decide between Paul and another beau named Jim. Kitty met Jim while the two of them were in college at East Carolina in Greenville, North Carolina. Jim was from the little town of LaGrange in Pitt County. Kitty said he was a cute little fellow but so too was Paul. Kitty recalls she just had to choose between Jim and Paul. She had already met and liked Jim's parents. Finally, Paul won the flip of the coin. Paul and Kitty went steady for several years. Kitty fell in love not only with Paul but also North Street.

We talked at length about life on North Street. Paul was one of the boys from North Street in Varina   His parents were Herman and Pearl Tutor. They lived just across the street from my parents and were good friends. Paul was a couple of years older than me. My first recollection of him was during his time in the military. He was stationed in South Korea. Like the Tyndalls, the Tutors lived in the shadow of Annie Atkins. Mrs. Akins owned our house and the Tutor's house. Kitty remembered those wonderful backyard BBQs at the home of Louise and Nelson Meadows. Kitty, with her winning smile and personality, soon won the hearts of the folks on North Street.

Kitty shared with me the story of her mother courting her father. Kitty's mother had moved to the Apex area to teach school. Mr. Johnson's mother rented rooms to the new teachers in the area. Kitty's Dad took the teachers to church just to be nice to them. According to Mr. Johnson, Kitty's mother tricked him into helping her with her pocketbook. He held it for her while she got in and out of the car. Mr. Johnson said Kitty's mother was quite able to exit the car on her own. He said she just wanted him to get close to her. Paul won the hand of Kitty. However, the town of Fuquay-Varina was the real winner because Kitty taught school in Fuquay-Varina for many years and was much beloved. Kitty is a superb Bridge player and plays in many clubs. She always enjoyed conversations with her many friends and had that winning smile for everyone.

Elsie and Roy Wilson:

Have you ever met a person whose laugh was infectious? That would be Elsie Wilson. She was always upbeat and always had funny stories to tell. Nothing got the best of her. During the 1950s, she and Roy and their daughter Priscilla (Snooks) lived just behind us. Snooks had a pony, and we rode it a lot. His name was Charlie, just like Nelson Meadows' monkey. Ole Charlie had three good legs; the fourth one was shorter than the others making for a unique ride with a certain dipping motion. Elsie and my mother were good friends. Roy was more reserved than Elsie. He worked for Clarence Hare at Varina Barber Shop where I got my first haircut. Roy said it was free, but I do not remember any of that.

There was also Mrs. Florence Curl. She ran the local beauty shop in Varina. Roy was from Asheville, North Carolina. He had twin sisters who came to visit from time to time. They could play the accordion and sing. When they came to town, there was always a BBQ chicken dinner for the neighborhood with live music. Like Odell Smith, Elsie could make the greatest fudge and shared it with all of us.

Worta and Jarvis Stephenson:

They lived next door and were just always there. I played in the lower portion of their back yard. Even though it was just beside my house, it seemed like I was miles from home. Worta was the medical nurse for the block. She had cures for ringworm, night cough, constipation, and trench mouth, none of which were pleasant. Worta said everybody needed a good cleaning out after a long, cold winter. Caster oil would do the trick. Once, Worta and Jarvis moved to the "Sally Farm" for a season of tenant farming. I am not sure where that was even though I visited the place. Tom and I were invited to spend a week on that farm in the middle of nowhere. What fun we had playing "hide and seek" in what seemed to me to be an endless, vast, dark forest? Jarvis was in the lumber business. At their house on North Street, they had two below-ground goldfish pools filled with whatever Jarvis caught on his many fishing trips. The Stephensons had two sons, Edgar and David, who were always as ready for an adventure with me.

Emma Lee and Mary Gladys

I really do not know where to stop when remembering the folks who made a difference in my life because so many people influenced my life in those early days in positive ways. I will always be grateful to my two aunts in Richmond, Emma Lee and Mary Gladys. They helped me get through college. When they came to North Carolina for a visit, it was a big treat. They were not wealthy, but I do remember the windows in their houses when raised would remain open with no sticks to hold them up. I thought it was magical since our windows on North Street required a stick to keep them open. We had a short stick for winter, and a long one for summer.

While attempting to remember all the people who touched my life in those early years, I am sure I have left someone out. Please know this was not intentional. When thinking back to the early years, it is quite possible that I have recalled events and times incorrectly; again, this was never intended to deceive but, as I have said many times, this is the way I remembered those days. I take full responsibility if I have misstated anything.

Chapter Nine – Special People of Willow Springs

James Fish

Almost anyone living around Willow Springs probably knows James. He is somewhat like myself, a self-appointed unofficial historian of the area. He has many recollections of his life here in Willow Springs and is always willing to share his stories. His family name has many trees, branches, and roots throughout Willow Springs and Panther Branch Township. When he and I met at the Fuquay-Varina Museum early in 2019, he was able to confirm some of the material I have used in this book. For example, James confirmed the mystery of Cannon Grove. He said it was a collection point for low-grade iron ore rocks around the area. He recalled the rocks were then taken to Fayetteville, North Carolina, where they were smelted into iron for Civil War cannon balls. James recalled the time when many of the roads around Willow Springs were paved and straightened. The year was 1948. James said much of the entire country was in need of repairs due to the war years.

Fred Fish

Fred, like James, knows many things about Willow Springs and freely shared them with me. He was the first person to tell me about Old Stage Coach house, the Adams Dairy, his own restored house, and much more. Over the past several years, my good friend, Fred Fish, and I have had many conversations about life and times around Willow Springs. Fred has lived around these parts most of his life. He is the oldest son of D. H. and Notie Fish. He was the first to tell me the Cannon Grove mystery. He recalled it may have been a plantation site, a school, a church, a collection point for low-grade iron ore to be used by the Confederates in making cannon balls—maybe it was all these things. In November

2013, more light was shed on the Cannon Grove mystery. The mystery first started with me as I pondered why there was a North Carolina highway sign at the intersection of highway 210 and Old Stage Road pointing to the location of Cannon Grove, 8 miles east. I talked with the folks at the North Carolina Highway Commission, but they could not tell me where Cannon Grove was located. Sometimes, when you think more polishing of that old broken mirror will not reveal anything new, a clear reflection slowly appears.

While talking to Fred Fish, my partner in the mystery quest, the conversation came back around to Cannon Grove. Fred took me to post station 3275 along highway 42 east. From my house on Bud Lipscomb Rd., turn left onto Old Stage, continue to highway 42, then right on 42 toward Clayton. About 100 yards down 42 on the left side is a brick ranch-style house. The house is about 50 yards down a winding dirt path. Just behind the house is what Fred said was the old building of Cannon Grove. The general description fit the building. The building is in need of repair and is currently being used for a storage barn. Unless the building gets some repairs soon it will disappear like so many other treasures and mysteries in my beloved Willow Springs. Fred further stated the Cannon Grove building was moved to its present location about 1950. The mover was Charlie Adams. He planned for it to be a residence for his wife and himself. A topographic map of churches in Wake county does indeed show Cannon Grove Church marked "Historical" and located on USGS topographic map at elevation 325 feet above sea level 35.554 degrees North and 78.692 degrees West.

Fred shared many facts about Willow Springs that were unknown to me. He recalled the old Adams Dairy on John Adams Road. He told me about the old school bus at Fellowship Presbyterian Church. He talked about his own house and the house's twin. Fred helped me clear up the mystery of what happened to the Old Stage Manor House. Fred said "It was sold to Willie York and the timbers were reused at his house in Raleigh." Through the years,

Fred has always been there to answer my questions. I think Fred loves Willow Springs as much as I do.

Fred recalls that the young people at Fellowship Presbyterian Church used the old school bus as a Sunday School classroom. This bus, commonly called a "woody" after its paneled wood exterior, was parked permanently in back of the little white plank church and, according to Fred Fish, the "ole woody" was never moved. Fred recalled the time period as about 1948/49. The teacher sat in the driver's seat while the young people in that class sat in the seats behind the driver. On a visit with L. P. Myatt at his garage in January 2014, he also confirmed Fred's story. His recollection was the vehicle was a small bus or an old station wagon. I wonder what happened to that old piece of history. Fred recalled the Fellowship Presbyterian Church building had no indoor plumbing. There was a hand-dug outhouse located on the back side of the property. I am told it came complete with a half-moon carving in the door and a Sears Catalog.

W. Irving Rowland and Tyson Bowden on Willow Springs' Liquor Store

Back in 1972, Ruth Holland Hardman interviewed Mr. W. Irving Rowland, a resident of Willow Springs. Here is his story as written by Ruth Hardman and remembered by Mr. Rowland:

"In my boyhood days there was a dispenser store on the dirt road near what is now Mrs. Carl Bennett's home. In those times it was legal to sell alcohol if you paid the tax revenue on it. It was often called the toddy tax. Mr. Rowland further recalled a man had drunk too much and did not realize that it was not a good idea to take a nap on the railroad tracks just behind the liquor store. He tried it and a train came along cutting off both his legs. Using a door from the dispensary store as an operating table Drs. James Judd Sr. and J. J. McCullers performed emergency surgery in the dispenser store building. Mr. Rowland witnessed the operation (every bloody detail) and said that the man survived the ordeal and lived for a long time afterward." [59]

There were no further reports on his drinking or napping habits.

In October 2015, I had an interview with Mr. Tyson Bowden. He too recalled a liquor store in Willow Springs. Mr. Bowden's account placed the store at the residence of Marshall Partin. The store was divided into two parts. One part contained a general merchandise store supplying the usual items of flour, corn meal, canned vegetables and bulk supplies of coffee and sugar. "If my memory is correct," said Mr. Bowden, "the other side of the store was for whiskey by the drink." No children were allowed on that side of the store. This was a perfectly legal operation so long as the tax was paid on the alcohol. Mr. Bowden said the general store on the other side had a barrel of brown sugar. When he was a young boy, Mr. Partin let him and other children dip out the brown sugar to eat as a treat. When the barrel got low, he turned it on its side and let the children crawl in and get to the hardened brown sugar at the bottom of the barrel. In his excitement to get to the brown sugar, the barrel rolled right through the door ending up in the middle of the ABC store. "My daddy was plenty mad at me but he soon forgot the whole thing."

Willow Springs, being the small area that it was, makes it logical to believe that the ABC store in Mrs. Hardman's account and the ABC store of Mr. Bowden's account are one and the same. Prohibition in 1910 ended all these sales. However, the memories linger on for some of us. "The liquor revenue (called the toddy tax) was a mainstay of school budgets throughout the county from 1880 until 1914. Prohibition caused such a financial crisis in 1909 that the school term was shortened, especially in the black schools where private funds were not forthcoming."[60]

George Francis: Matters of Myatt's Mill

These recollections came from George Francis, Jr. while spending an afternoon talking about his love for Willow Springs. George said, "located at intersection of Panther Lake Road and Old Stage Road was a milling company operated by George R. Francis Senior (his father). The Mill was leased by Mr. Francis in December 1945. The operation lasted sixteen years from 1945 through 1961. The mill offered water-ground corn meal for people and a variety of corn and wheat-based animal feeds. The mill located at Panther Branch dam featured a large horizontal water wheel. The wheel and grinding stones are still on the property (2019) and located under the millhouse. The dam has been repaired and improved several times over the years, but the mill operation for George's dad was moved to Varina in 1961. Some of this information was obtained from an ad in the 1957 annual yearbook for Willow Springs Elementary School.[61]

In my many e-mail conversations with my old high school classmate, George Francis Jr., he said a mill was in operation at Myatt's Mill Pond since the 1860s. I think the mill operations are much older than that. Perhaps as far back as 1790. George said the first mill was built and operated by members of the early Myatt families in our area. Later Myatt's Mill, the pond and the store were owned by Elder T. Floyd Adams. Still later a Doctor Poe from Chapel Hill leased or purchased the lake from Mr. Adams. Dr. Poe then drained the pond to cut the stumps out so he could convert it into a water-skiing facility. George said he had memories of folks coming with wash-tubs to scoop up the large fish flopping around in the deep holes when the pond was drained. The folks scooping up those fish were in a perfect position to tell everyone how large the fish were. Oral histories report some bass at twenty pounds. One account said they had a catfish that weighed thirty pounds. With no one able to prove them wrong, the actual size of the fish scooped up just got bigger and bigger. You can be the judge on how true the stories were.

George and I graduated from high school in 1960. After graduation he worked in the radio industry. His job, coupled with his military service, took him all over the world. When we reconnected much later, we discovered we both loved the history of Willow Springs. On November 18, 2015, we spent a day together just riding around my little Willows with George pointing out places and events while I asked questions and quickly took notes. Here are a few of the nuggets he told me.

As it turns out, George Jr. also has written about his time living in Willow Spring and other places highlighting his family connection to "sharecropping." His father, George Sr., came to Willow Springs about 1945 when he leased the grist mill at Myatt's Mill. The name was changed to Francis Feed Mill. Before 1945, his family were sharecroppers working the land for half the profit while the land owner kept the books and most of the proceeds. George Jr.'s mother was Katie Stephenson. She was sister to A. T. Stephenson who ran a store, first at Myatt's Mill and later on highway 42. I remember Miss Katie when she managed the cafeteria at Willow Springs Elementary School.

George said his mother was a very brave farm woman. Once while breastfeeding his little brother, Larry, a large black snake slithered into the house attracted by the aroma of the breast milk. George recalled, "my mother told me not to move" as she got up and slowly reached for her handy hatchet. With one whack, she separated the snake from its head. All this time she was holding onto little Larry. After the ambush, she sat back down and calmly continued the feeding.

As we rode down Mount Pleasant Church Road, George recalled he had two mules as pets, named Kate and Charlie. When Charlie died in 1950, they buried him in a field feet up. He showed me the exact spot. Sometimes you get more information than needed. It still makes for great storytelling.

George showed me the site where a crop duster plane crashed at the intersection of Jackson King Road and Mt. Pleasant Road. It happened in the summer of 1952. This was very near the old homeplace of Moses and Henrietta Dupree. The plane hit a tree in the field, and the tree survived. The pilot was not so lucky. George told me about Gene Bennett Barbour and the band he led back in the fifties called "Gene and the Cavaliers." Gene and the band are still remembered at "The Rock and Roll Hall of Fame" in Ohio. Gene is one of those lucky Willow Springs boys who made it big.

According to information from George Francis Jr., there was a large snake that crossed Panther Lake every summer evening about sunset. Folks came from miles around to watch this reptile make his daily swim to the boathouse. That story made the news and was reported in the "News" and "Observer." George also recalled another story about a road gang of convict prisoners that escaped while working near the Myatt's millhouse. One of these convicts hid in the water of the lake using a reed to breathe. No word on the final outcome of this escape. George further stated "there are dozens of springs in all those woods around the lake. Some have water so clear and cold, it will give you a headache. North of the lake there are springs connected all the way up to and past highway 42." George said there were minks in the headwaters of the lake as late as the 1950s. I believe this story as I saw otters in Bass Lake headwaters about 1957. At that time, the lake was owned by the father of Richard Ellis, another classmate. I spent many summer days swimming in the lake and exploring the headwaters.

George mentioned that one of the old mill stones in the yard of Tyson Bowden probably came from the grist mill at Myatt's Mill pond. The woods between Mount Pleasant Road and Old Stage Road where the bridge over Black Creek crosses is where there are several Indian mounds back in the woods. I think that land belongs to the Weeks family.

Another story told by George involved two girls who lived near the intersection of Old Stage Road and Barbour Store Road. George drove a school bus back then, around 1957. It seems the school board discovered the girls were, in fact, Native American. George recalled one of the girls was named Daisy Hudson. The school board stopped him from picking them up. I can believe this as North Carolina operated three separate school systems at that time. I have often wondered whatever happened to those two girls.

Like so much of Willow Springs, there are kinships everywhere. George is related to the Stephensons and the Ogburns. He regularly attends the reunions of both. Spending the day with George was a pleasure for me.

Billy Ray Yeargan

Mr. Hurley Dupree owned a grinding mill. His milling operation was open for several years grinding corn and wheat for local farmers in exchange for a portion of their product. The acceptable rate was that the miller got one bushel for every twenty brought in for grinding. Albert Partin operated this mill. I am assuming the mill was owned by Hurley Dupree. The mill was located down below Myatts Mill near Bill Love's place on Black Creek in Wake County. This information was given to me during an interview with Billy Ray Yeargan on May 5, 2015. Billy recalls that T. Floyd Adams and Charlie Adams operated a cotton gin about 1922 along Panther Lake road at or near the intersection of Old Stage Road.

The following information was taken from an account by Mr. T. Floyd Adams reflecting on this business venture. "He was the manager for the first year or so. He was 28 years old when he started working at the gin. The year was 1922. He and his business partner, Mr. J. W. Blalock, who was considered to be the wealthiest man in Panther Branch Township, together with his nephew Charlie Adams approached T. Floyd and offered to furnish all the equipment and capital if T. Floyd would manage the day-to-day operations. In return for his service, he would receive one half the annual proceeds. T. Floyd accepted the offer. In those early years he earned $300 for ginning season (about a four-month time period). Later T. Floyd Adams became an investor in the gin. They borrowed $30,000 dollars to finance a new three-stand system operated by an oil engine. T. Floyd became a successful business man and expanded his business interest in other fields. T. Floyd said "At the age of forty-four I was encouraged by the leaders of Panther Branch Township to be a candidate for county commissioner of Wake County. I confess that little persuasion was needed since I have always been interested in government. I was elected and continued in this office for 16 years."[62] No information was provided as to how long this gin was in business.

Bryant Tyndall: The Church Fire

Fellowship Baptist Church in Willow Springs was the site of a tragic fire in the wee morning hours of September 13, 1990. The building and most of its contents were destroyed. Somehow, I just cannot forget that tragic night and that devastating fire at Fellowship Baptist Church. That church was then and is today (2021) my church. That is why I have chosen to include this event in my collection of stories even if it is out of the time frame.

During the early hours of September 13, 1990, Judy, Patrick (our youngest son), and I were awakened by a phone call from Susan Harvell, another church member, telling us of the fire. We drove two miles to the church in time to see the fire reach above the tree line; we knew this was serious. The massive fire raged above the kitchen wing of the church. As we stood in disbelief still clinging to the hope that somehow the sanctuary could be saved, we were sickened to see flames shooting from the overhangs around the sanctuary. It was not long before that too was engulfed in a fiery finish. I recall a small group of members stood in disbelief that hot September night trying to make sense of this tragedy. Several commented that the cross atop the sanctuary would be the last to fall, and it was. At that moment, we were confused and saddened by our loss. Lots of questions were asked, but the thing I remember most was the closeness of the members. We cried, hugged each other, and firmly resolved to rebuild. According to reports appearing in the local paper, a neighbor reported the fire at 1:37 am Thursday. When firemen arrived shortly after, the building was fully engulfed with the flames. Some 25 firefighting units from nine area fire stations responded. It took four hours to bring the fire under control. There was little left of the building or its contents.

The following Sunday worship services were held at Suggs Funeral Home in Fuquay-Varina and were later moved to the facilities of a private school on the Wake Chapel Christian Church property in Fuquay-Varina. Services remained there until the new church building was completed. The loss was valued at $570,000 with insurance providing a portion and the members raising the rest. Rev. Jim Aycock said offers of help poured into the church from all over. Churches across Wake County contributed to the Fellowship Church building fund. "Folks and churches of this area have been wonderful," Rev. Aycock said.[63]

By May of 1993, the loan allowing for the rebuilding of the church had been repaid in full. Senior Pastor R. Jay Waggoner said the event was "another step in completing the task for which God has called us." The note burning symbolizing the end of indebtedness for the Fellowship congregation was part of the thirtieth annual homecoming service for that year.

Siddy Honeycutt and the Watkins Man

As one of the many oral histories I have collected over the years, the story of Oscar Paul Honeycutt and wife, Siddy, come to mind. They lived on Highway 55 at the intersection of Old Honeycutt Road. Their two-story farmhouse has been torn down and a new

BP station is on the site now. Aunt Siddy loved to bake cakes for Sunday lunch. Everyone was always invited to her house. The number of guests was not important. Saturday was always the day she baked cakes for the big Sunday lunch. This story comes to me from her daughter, Flora Mangum. "One Saturday morning, the Watkins man, a well-known traveling salesman, had just made his regular monthly visit. He left Aunt Siddy with her usual order of rubbing liniment, vanilla flavoring, and other items. In her haste to get on with the baking, Aunt Siddy left the entire order on the kitchen table. As she rushed to put her cakes together, she accidentally put the Watkins rubbing liniment in the cake batter instead of the vanilla flavoring. The next day a revival preacher from Kennebec Baptist Church was among the invited guests and, as usual, he was the first to sample the cakes and ate the most. He was very kind and said nothing about the strange taste. Later, that day as others tasted her pretty desserts, it was discovered that the strange taste came from the rubbing liniment, not the vanilla flavoring. Siddy said, "I never did like that preacher anyway, but I don't want to go to hell for killing a man of God." Nothing was ever said about the preacher making a return trip for lunch. The revival continued for the next week. My guess is that he was careful about what and where he ate.

Mary Honeycutt Stokes: Trading Eggs for Candy

My Aunt Mary Stokes told me a story of a young girl, Mary, who lived in the Duncan area a few miles to the west of Willow Springs. She said they moved around a lot in those days, sharecropping tobacco with different landowners. Mary and her little brother Clifton always wanted candy but the family rarely had money to buy it. She and Clifton would take eggs in a basket down the railroad tracks to the local store. The Tutors, who were the storeowners, would trade the eggs for candy. She further said she could never figure out the system but the candy was always good. As she remembers it took fewer eggs for the candy in the winter months than in the spring time. Her mother explained that the chickens laid more eggs in the spring and the old "supply and demand" theory went into effect. According to the latest poultry data, a chicken in the prime of her life lays an egg every 28 hours. (With or without the help of the rooster). I wonder if anyone has told the chickens about all this.

Paul Honeycutt: There is a Cat in the Well

My great uncle Paul told me many stories about those cold winter mornings and having to break the ice in the water bucket to get the first drink of the day. His first morning job was to fire up the wood cookstove in the kitchen with kindling wood. He said the family dogs and several cats all slept together near the warm space under the kitchen stove. His wife told me of the time a cat fell into their well. The cat drowned quickly but remained in the well for several days before being discovered. The Honeycutts were without well water for several months while sulphur, lime, and Clorox were poured into the well each day. I don't recall how long they waited, but, to this day, I look for a dead cat in a well before taking that first drink. At last report everyone lived through the cat episode except for that poor cat.

Daisy Lipscomb: Best Biscuits and Other Cool Stuff

(Interview 12/2/70) Aunt Daisy, as we called her, is remembered fondly for her sharp wit and pleasant personality. She was the only person I ever knew who could bend down, touch her toes and never bend her knees. If you think that is easy just try it. And she could do it at age 80. She always liked to show us how it was done. I will never forget those good old days with Aunt Daisy. She and husband Bud lived two houses up from the Tyndalls on Bud Lipscomb Road. She once told me she knew how to "talk the fire out of folks with burns." On one occasion, I burned my hand. She did talk the fire out of my hand while rubbing my arm and saying some words I could not understand. I am not saying I believe in her special brand of magic, but I did recover after she uttered those secret words and my burned fingers stopped hurting. I pleaded with her to tell me the secret words. She said she could not tell me what she did. She said telling would break the spell and she would lose the gift. Aunt Daisy said the secret words were passed down to only special children of latter generations and she was one of those special granddaughters.

Aunt Daisy and I had many conversations over the years. She told me several stories of how she and Mr. Bud (her husband) were among the first to grow tobacco on a large scale in this area. Mr. Bud would take country hams to many of the tobacco buyers. Sometimes that helped the crop sell higher. She told me of the many families coming to Willow Springs from Granville County to grow tobacco. She talked lovingly of her three boys: Clyde, William, and David. She said Mr. Bud wanted to give each of them a farm to help them get started in life. I asked if she had other children and she replied "O yes. I had several that were stillborn or died in infancy. Mr. Bud would never say where he buried them but did assure me they were in a place never to get wet."

When I moved to Willow Springs circa 1963, Mr. Bud was very sick and spent most of his days in a hospital bed on their glassed-in side porch. She cared for him during all those days with little or no outside help. His pet name for her was "Duck." Duck answered every call promptly. If she complained, I never heard it. Daisy married young at age fifteen. Mr. Bud was a few years older than Daisy. Aunt Daisy died in 1975 and so did a lot of her wonderful stories. I only wish I had asked her more questions.

On many occasions folks from all over came by her house for Sunday lunch. She never knew how many folks would show up, but she never ran out of food. She could make the best biscuits I ever tasted. If the biscuit supply got low, she would pop up in middle of the meal, still dressed in her Sunday best, and make another pan full in record time using only one hand. Daisy was sister to Henry A. Smith. Henry Smith was my step-father-in-law. The old Lipscomb home place is still standing and is now owned by her grandson. The house has been lovingly restored and is today a showplace in our area, especially during Christmas.

David and Angela, I think she would be proud of both of you and the house.

Annie Mae Adams: The Fire at John Quinton Adams Home

It is a rare but delightful treat when you get another small piece of that elusive history of Willow Springs allowing you a sketchy glimpse back to the Mount Pleasant community on a warm spring evening in 1901. This is just a portion of the entire article quoting Mrs. Annie Mae Adams

"I was nine years old. We lived in a two-story house with the kitchen at the back separated from the main dwelling. We ate supper in the kitchen that night. My sister Nelia, who was seventeen, had cooked the meal. After supper we all returned to the main house and I retired for bed early. John Quinton, my father, had also retired early that evening with a headache. The younger children including myself were readying for bed when someone alerted the family to a fire in the attached kitchen of our house. Back then there were no fire departments in the country like there are today. The wind was blowing from the kitchen toward the main house. Mr. and Mrs. Adams along with children Nelia, Charlie, Lonnie and Cleveland did what they could with a bucket brigade from the well to the house. Annie and John were too little to help. Climbing a ladder to the roof two stories up, the water did little to stop the flames. Soon neighbors came to help. All was to no avail; the fire soon overtook the main house and by evening sunset the Adams house would be gone. Each time they extinguished a spot, the fire would reappear. They were fighting a losing battle. The men then cut a hole in the roof from the inside and were able to get to the hotspots quicker. This too was a lost cause. When those fighting the fire realized that they were going to lose the house, they started going inside taking furniture and other possessions out. Nelia went upstairs to her room for some items. Mother soon became anxious and sent Charlie to check on her. The two of them just made it out in time. My father's sister, Susanah Adams and her husband, Uncle Jim, took us in for night. The next day was Sunday and there wasn't anything left but a pile of ashes. The house was rebuilt by the next year's end for the grand sum of one hundred round dollars in labor only. Mr. Davis from Benson did the work and was the person who had built the first house fifty years earlier."

The house that was rebuilt still stands today, although remodeled some, along Hwy 42 about 3 miles east of Willow Springs facing John Adams Road and the Adams winery. According to Johnny Adams III, grandson of John Quinton Adams, and Joyce, his Mother, "his grandmother, Annie Eliza Blalock Adams had inherited from her father, Hugh Blalock, just the year before the fire, a tract of timber containing the last of the old growth of longleaf pines in the area. Those pines were cut for the construction of the house. Her brother, Bill Blalock, operated a saw mill and processed all the lumber that was used in the framing. It was all heart pine. He offered his services for free. The flooring and moldings were purchased from Briggs Hardware Store in Raleigh. It has been estimated the total cost of the almost 4,000 square foot structure was about $500 excluding the moldings and flooring." That had to be the deal of century.[64] This information comes from a newspaper article in the Fuquay-Varina Independent February 24, 2010.

The preceding was a transcript of a taped recording made by Annie Akins remembering a fire at her parent's home in Willow Springs, N.C. The recording was made in 1985, nine months before her death at age 94. The recording has been lovingly edited and transcribed by her daughter, Willa Akins Adcock. This recording was published in the Fuquay-Varina Independent on Wednesday, February 24, 2010. Many thanks must go out to Willa Adcock for her care and preservation of the events long ago and forgotten by many of us.

Annie Eliza Blalock: General Sherman's March Through Willow Springs

These recollections were also written down by Annie Mae Adams Akins in 1985. Mrs. Akins was born in Willow Springs and was a long-time property owner and resident of Varina. She died October 27, 1985 at the age of 94. I will always be thankful to my friend Willa Akins Adcock (her daughter) who transcribed this tape and submitted it to our online newspaper. Willa Adcock has spent many hours editing this information. Her efforts have made it possible for me to get another one of those little glimpses back in time.

The following is a recollection of a story told by Annie Mae Adams Akins, recounting the story told by her mother, Annie Eliza Blalock, remembering the time when General Sherman's troops were coming through Willow Springs in the spring of 1865. Annie Eliza's parents were Christiana and Hugh Blalock.

"In April of 1865 my mother Annie Eliza Blalock was 9 years old when General William T. Sherman's army came marching and plundering through Willow Springs. Everyone knew the Northern Brigade was coming because stories of their violent actions and foraging were preceding them as they marched. The Blalock family heard that the troops would be coming by way of Old Stage Road from Clemons (now known as Clayton) on their way to Raleigh from the battle of Bentonville. General Sherman and his troops had marched from Savannah, Georgia, to Bentonville, N.C. This march has been described as 'total war' because the Federal troops destroyed as they marched. Sherman's troops burned cities, homes and farm buildings on a wide scale; something the Southern General Robert E. Lee, never did. Sherman's army caused untold suffering for generations to come. General Joseph E. Johnston had met and been defeated by General Sherman's men at Bentonville on March 19-21 1865. The federal army had 60,000 troops; Johnson, the Southern general, had 20,000. Johnson withdrew to Smithfield as the Northern battalion marched on to Goldsboro."

Hugh Rias Blalock and his wife Christina had a home about a half mile from Old Stage Road on what is today Hwy 42 East, about two miles from Willow Springs. Stories had preceded these troops of Tecumseh Sherman as they advanced; stories abounded about how they destroyed civilian property and laid waste to everything that might help the South continue fighting. The Blalock family had heard how Sherman's renegades destroyed railroads by burning the cross ties and then heating the rails and bending them around trees making them unusable. They heard how they built bonfires with the split rail fences used for keeping the animals corralled on the farm. The Blalock family was alarmed, but they were preparing for the arrival of this devastating army. Having much to hide, each member knew they had precious little time before the Yankee army would arrive in the Willow Springs area from Goldsboro.

Annie Eliza and her 8 siblings, along with their parents and a few trusted slaves, set about burying the special things, all except Grandpa Hugh's gold which he buried himself. The horses and mules were put in a low meadow near the creek and the cows were tied in a reed swamp beyond the pasture. William "Bill" Blalock, my mother's brother, was 12 at the time and a true rebel. He had a colt that he loved and was training. He took additional care to hide him well; he did not want his colt to be found by the marauding soldiers. They buried the cured hams, sausage, and other meat as well as the lard from the hog killings. They hid all the produce they had grown: potatoes, dried apples, nuts, dried peas, beans, and also the vegetables they had canned. They even hid the chickens. When the Union army arrived at the Blalock farm, the soldiers went immediately to Atlas, an older trusted slave; they told him they were his friends and had come to set him free along with all the other slaves. They asked Atlas to show them where everything was hidden. Atlas refused. Alexander, age 17, told them where everything was hidden. The soldiers took everything including Bill's prized colt.

Grandpa Hugh Blalock was sitting on his front porch and saw all that was happening. A soldier came up to him and said, "Alexander tells me you have gold hidden" pressing a gun to his head. The soldier said, "Tell me where it is or I will shoot you right now." Grandpa said without flinching "Shoot! I am just as ready to die as I will ever be." Remarkably, the Yankee soldier did not shoot; he put his gun away and went with the other mercenaries into the house. They took several feather-bed comforters, clothing and anything else of interest. After rummaging through the property and hanging around for a couple of days, those ruffians left with all the wagons and carts loaded. They tied feather beds to several of the wagons and slit the ticking so the goose down would be forced to fly out in the wind. As the soldiers raced down the road the feathers were drifting out and up as they continued on their north-bound journey. Annie Eliza said "the feathers from the eiderdown comforters floated up into the air and they very slowly twirled around as they descended. As the white downy feather settled in the nearby fields turning everything around an eerie white; it looked like it had been snowing. These feathers, much like the lives of the people of the South, were at a loss as to where they might finally settle. Yet, time would reveal that it was never to be gathered again. Perhaps an image of what was happening to a way-of-life in the Old South."[65]

Mary Elizabeth Smith: Sherman's March

Another time Sherman's army approached Willow Springs, Mary Elizabeth Smith's great-grandmother's home was also in the path of Sherman's army. "It was the spring of 1864, the family tells of her Grandma's mother (Amelia Rand) who was a large woman and her husband, who was rather slightly built. The weight disparity was so great, their carriage had to be reinforced to correct the imbalance. Grandma was four years old when the Yankees came through Wake County. To protect the food in their storeroom, her mother (Amelia) planted all her bulk of over 250 pounds on two barrels in front of the door and dared the Yankee Captain to pass. While Amelia was so occupied, she had to suffer the indignity of watching her four-year old daughter play happily on the lap of this

Yankee Captain." [66]

Susie Adams: Life on a Willow Springs Farm

When Susie Adams was 90 years old, she wrote some facts about life on a farm in Willow Springs. She died two years later in 1981. Before her death, Susie gave her first cousin, Annie Mae Adams Akins, a copy of her notes. Before Annie Mae died in 1985, she passed the notes to her daughter, Willa Akins Adcock. After editing the old notes and adding some remembrances of her own childhood while visiting at the Willow Springs home place. Willa Adcock wrote an account of these events for the local online newspaper.

"Susie recalled her early years living on a 213-acre farm in southern Wake County three miles east of Willow Springs. Her ancestors came from Virginia. Susie's grandfather, "Jack," moved to the house she had lived in back in 1863. Susie had three sisters: Roetta, Valie, Beatrice, and a brother who died in infancy. In those early years, she went to a public school located near home. It was a one-room one-teacher school. The school term was about five months. After finishing school, probably at the Mount Pleasant school in the area, she went to Raleigh to BUW Baptist University for Women 1904-1909. That school later became Meredith College.

"Susie recalled her father was a farmer, teacher and 'justice of the peace' for the county and many court cases were almost always settled in their home. Sometimes one or the other of the clients would acquire a lawyer from Raleigh. That would draw a crowd to hear how the dispute would be settled. Many times, someone would want to fight, but her father would not permit it. He would emphatically say "No," and he would not allow any profane language either. He did a lot of public work along with the farm work and teaching. Susie often wondered how he did so many things and kept going.

She always liked the farm life. Being born on a farm, she knew much about the many ups and downs of farm life. After her father died, they did not plant wheat or cane any longer. The four sisters lived together at their home place. Susie, Valie, Beatrice, and Roetta were in charge of planting the crops of corn, cotton, and sweet potatoes. They would hire a boy or man to do the plowing, and they did the rest of the work. Usually in August they would pull the fodder from the cornstalks and tie it into bundles to dry. If it looked like rain, they hastened to get the fodder in the barn by driving the horse hitched to the buggy—yes, hitched to a buggy. The horse would not pull a wagon. What a sight to see with the horse going across the field pulling that buggy.

The next job in the harvest cycle was the laborious task of picking cotton. The cotton was picked from the burrs on the stalk by hand. The cotton was then put in large bags. It took long days to fill the bags. At day's end, there were plenty of sore fingers. The sisters were always glad to finish but, when they got caught up with their harvesting, they would help some of the neighbors who had larger farms.

After the cotton was picked, it was hog-killing time. Everyone enjoyed the homemade pork chops, sausage, and all the fresh meats. The neighbors would fill the large wash pot with water, heat it, and put it into a barrel. They would then kill the hogs, scald them, put them on a wood floor of sorts, clean them, and scrape them to remove the hair. Next, they would hang the hogs up to cut them into the different parts. With this done, it wouldn't be long before they could begin cooking. They always had plenty of fruits including apples, peaches, plums, berries, and grapes which allowed them to make jams and jellies. Yes, it was a busy time and much work to be done, but they enjoyed those happy days."[67]

Anna Jones Stephens: Life in Willow Springs

Mrs. Stephens was 78 when she commented on life in Willow Springs in an article appearing in The Raleigh Times December 26, 1983.[68] "I came to Willow Springs in October 1926, to teach music at the community school." It was "brand new," she said. She and the other teachers boarded in a big white house near the school. Mrs. Stephens's friend, Doris Messer, who later moved away from Willow Springs, recollected that "we picked cotton for 30 cents a hundred pounds."[69] "In those days, we did not have any paved roads," said Mrs. Stephens, who lived within a rock's throw of the school. Mrs. Stephens met her husband, Hoke, who ran a general merchandise store in Willow Springs until 1966, a year before his death. Hoke Stephens built a new store building when N. C. Highway 42 was paved and came through years ago. "Candy was a penny and Coke cost a nickel," she recalled. Back then, the Willow Springs Post Office was in a private home, and Hoke Stephens was in charge of tossing the mail bag onto the train when it rolled through town once or twice a day. Passenger service ended in the late 1930s. Mrs. Stephens said the community was bigger now with more people, and she didn't know everybody the way she once did. Would she ever consider leaving? "Lord, no. What you talking about? No sir," she exclaimed!

The Indians around Varina and Willow Springs

"When Europeans started arriving in southern Wake County, they encountered both Woodland and Mississippian Indians, but not in large permanent settlements. Only a few of their artifacts have survived the last two and a half centuries."[70] The Tuscarora Indians who occupied the Cape Fear region from the banks of the Cape Fear River east into what is now known as Greene County were probably the Indians they encountered. These Indians would have most likely been travelling through southern Wake County. They spoke an Iroquois dialect.

When John Lawson crossed through the Carolinas, he noted an Indian trading trail in what is now Willow Springs. This was later to become the general route of our highway 42. Lawson made camp in the area of Hillsboro along the banks of the Eno River and continued to follow an Indian trail making camp again in the Clayton area. Later he explored the area of Contentnia Creek in Greene County before arriving at the North Carolina Coast. [71]

In the book, A History of Fuquay-Varina, a reference to Indians living in the area of Piney Woods, later known as Fuquay Springs, is observed. "The exact name of the tribe was maybe Sippihaw or Sippahaw or Saxapahaw. The professionals who study Native American history can offer no written or archeological proof of who these people were. In honor of those people, Fuquay's first post office and later its first golf course were named Sippihaw." [72] Their permanent settlements were far to the east of Wake County. They were most likely Tuscaroran hunting parties just passing through southern Wake County. The one exception to this is the small band of the Native Americans called the Coharrie people. They were located in Harnett and Sampson Counties. It is thought these Indians descended from the aboriginal tribe of the Neusick Indians. The Coharrie were first to establish a subscription school in the Deep Run community in Sampson County.

The Tuscaroran war of 1702 slowed development in Southern Wake County even though the events of this war were 90 miles east in Greene County. It was in Greene County where 200 white settlers, men, women, and children were killed by the Tuscaroran Indians in two days. It took a long time for the population to bounce back. Folks in that time were just not sure if settlements in this dark corner of North Carolina would ever recover.

"In 1701 John Lawson found the Tuscarorans occupying fifteen towns with a fighting force of 1,200 warriors. Encroachment on their land and enslavement of the Indians led to the Tuscaroran Wars and the demise of the Tuscarorans in North Carolina. Tuscarora tradition claims that in early times the tribe possessed the country between the sea and the mountains. When first encountered by the white men, however, this tribe lived only along the banks of the Roanoke, Tar, Pamlico, and Neuse rivers." [73]

Mr. D. H. Baker: All about Indians

D. H. Baker was a local TV repairman (now deceased). He had an impressive collection of Indian artifacts, probably Tuscaroran, maybe Sippihaw, or maybe Neusick. He had a museum located at his home in Chalybeate Springs. He was always available for school groups and local folks, including myself, offering free-guided tours around his museum and his grounds collection. Mr. Baker always spoke kindly of these early inhabitants. His respect for these first North Carolinians was reverent as if he knew them personally. His knowledge of these early people was then and is now most impressive. He deserves a lot of recognition for his collecting skills.

Indians around the Eno River in Hillsborough, N. C. in present day Orange County established trading paths along middle creek and other waterways near Wake County. Many of those trading paths led across Panther Branch Township on the way to the East. "Often the Indian hunting parties passing through parts of Wake County would cut trees allowing them to fall pointing other hunting parties in the direction of our river crossings at probably the Neuse or the Cape Fear Rivers."[74]

Tyson Bowden: Life in Willow Springs

I visited Mr. Bowden in October of 2015. We had a great afternoon just talking about his life and times when he was just a young boy living with a large family of brothers and sisters in Willow Springs. Tyson served his country as a member of the United States Army. He said he was drafted just as the War in Europe was ending. He said, "There was still fighting in the Pacific and that is where I expected to go." He completed his basic training at Fort Jackson in South Carolina about 1945 and was trained to be a gunner. According to Mr. Bowden, that was the most dangerous position in the Army at that time. His first duty assignment was in Virginia and then on to New York City where he boarded a military transport bound for Lahar, France. For thirteen days and nights, he rarely left his bunk. He and every member in his little group were seasick. "I lost ten pounds, and I didn't care if the ship sank so long as it would stop moving up and down. Luckily for us that did not happen." Upon arriving in France, he was quickly sent to Munich, Germany by train in a box car. His group of about thirteen men were assigned duty in the German City of Vanberg. Tyson said it is funny now to think about those times.

"I had been to Raleigh before 1945 but never rode a train or been on a ship. There I was a little old farm boy from Willow Springs in France and later in Germany. I weighed 110 pounds and my rifle was bigger than me. While there, we set switches for the city's train systems."

Mr. Bowden and six other American G. I.'s provided box cars when needed to send American Military supplies and ration packages to other occupied German cities. Mr. Bowden said the German people were glad to see the Americans as they feared occupation by the Russian Army. While in Germany, he lived in a house with the other men. There were two German women who cooked and cleaned for them. He said he never pulled KP or made his bed. He always had three hot meals daily and a clean place to sleep. According to Mr. Bowden, the German people were just as tired of Hitler as the Americans were. He did comment that it was a shame there was so much destruction.

The train station/depot in Vanberg had a glass top dome. It was a thing of beauty in its day. When he arrived, there was only one glass panel left in the entire structure. The vibrations from all those bombs dropping caused the window glass to break. Mr. Bowden said he carried a 45-pistol strapped to his belt all the time. He only fired it once while testing a tracer bullet. The German population was under a city-wide curfew from 6pm to 6am. Anyone caught violating this restriction was sent to detention. He said detention was not a nice place to be sent as it was almost like a prison.

While commenting on his military time in Germany, he mentioned that cigarettes cost him about a dollar per carton at the PX and could be sold on the black market for $70. Mr. Bowden said, "We wired most of our money back home, keeping only a little bit to spend while over there. We found out pretty quick the German marc was about worthless." Mr. Bowden told me several times how proud he was to serve with the men he was assigned with. They helped each other out when they could. "Even today I try to stay in touch with these men." We only have four still alive today. J. D. Hall was one of the remaining four. (Oct 2015). Getting the chance to go on one of the freedom flights to Washington D.C. and see the World War II memorial was a great day for Mr. Bowden. He concluded his conversation about his military days by saying it was the best thing that ever happened to him.

Ray Bowden: A Visit to a Cotton Gin

Ray and his wife Betty are our friends here in Willow Springs. The Tyndalls and the Bowdens attend Fellowship Baptist Church. Ray recollected:

"I have spent my entire life around Willow Springs. My family tree grows deep, straight, and tall between the Pollards on my mother's side and the Bowden clan on the other side. My father and mother both came from large families producing lots of cousins, aunts, and uncles. Some of my early memories are rooted in my many trips with my father to other farms and mills around the area. On one such trip, we visited the new cotton gin operated by J. R. Woodward and T. Floyd Adams down at Myatt's Mill. They had just installed a new device capable of sucking the raw cotton up from the wagon and into the gin. Mr. Woodward once told me to stand in the middle of the wagon and when the sucking updraft was turned on, my hair stood straight up. It did not suck me up into the gin as promised, but it sure made a big impression on me."

Ray reminded me that Myatt's Mill was originally located further up Panther Branch just behind his present house. Some of the foundation still remains and, as a child, he used to play in the creek at that site. Ray recalled Charlie Adams, brother to John Q. Adams, moved an old building from its present location along Old Stage Road to his farm just east of Olive's Cash Store. Ray remembered Mr. Adams and his wife Blannie lived in that old building. The old building is still standing along highway 42.

Research has revealed to me that the old building is in fact Cannon Grove church or school and perhaps both. Ray further recalled a dairy operated by T. Floyd Adams and his son. The dairy operated along John Adams road just before the curve leading to the residence of Fred and Frances Fish. There is not much remaining to the Adams Dairy today, just a few foundation blocks of the old milking barn. The dairy did not stay in business very long and was closed before 1952.

Eula Smith Harris: Life in Willow Springs

Commenting on life in Willow Springs, Eula Smith Harris said, "I have lived in Willow Springs all my life and worked in the school cafeteria the last five years." She has the same warm feelings as Anna Jones Stephens when it comes to leaving the area. "There are people here in this community that I've known since we were children," she said. "My parents and theirs knew each other. My children and theirs know each other now. When one of my sons died five years ago, they helped me out. I wouldn't consider living anywhere else."[75]

Charles Strickland: Being a Postmaster in Willow Springs

In an article appearing in the newspaper, Mr. Strickland estimated the Willow Springs population at around 300 to 500 people. "Farming is the way most folks here make their living, although many are state employees and some work in Raleigh and Fuquay-Varina." There are several churches in the community and some businesses next to the post office and J.R Woodward's television repair shop. There is Willow Spring Service Center, owned by Leroy and Elsie Riley. The Riley's store is the farmer's meeting place, where all world news is discussed and all the world's problems are solved.[76]

Mrs. Hilda Pleasants: A Wonderful Telephone Conversation

My first conversations with Mrs. Pleasants were telephone inquiries I made. I wanted to make a positive identification for a name appearing in the 1915 session records of Fellowship Presbyterian Church. The writing in those documents had faded over the years. Vivian Page could have been the first person to join Fellowship Presbyterian Church after the charter roll call was completed in October, 1914. For this reason, I felt it was important to get more information about this lady. However, her name as recorded was not clearly written. I was referred to Mrs. Pleasants by her niece, Margaret Page Jones. Mrs. Pleasants was in sound mind and happy to share with me many things about Willow Springs. We talked for over one hour. Miss Hilda said the mystery name "Vivian Page," but back in 1914, folks called her Vivie and she was sister to Mr. Early Page. Miss Hilda did remember the old Jolly cemetery but did not know what happened to it. Miss Hilda also told me about another church involved in that early circuit of churches. It was Oakland Presbyterian, down in Johnston County. Miss Hilda talked for one hour; her memory of events back that far was amazing. I had hoped to visit her in the near future. I am sorry I did not go as I promised. She passed away in 2016.

Mrs. Kathleen Jones Ogburn Tunstall: September 12, 1981 Dr. White

While reflecting on the early history of Fellowship Presbyterian Church, Kathleen Ogburn Tunstall recalled, "Dr. White, the pastor of First Presbyterian Church in Raleigh, often visited with our little church. Mrs. Tunstall recalled he and others from the First Presbyterian Church in Raleigh aided in the formation of our early church. First Presbyterian Church in Raleigh looked upon its work at Fellowship Presbyterian Church as "home mission outreach into rural Wake County, a dark corner of the County." Dr. White and the First Presbyterian Church are mentioned fondly by some of our older members. Mrs. Kathleen Ogburn Tunstall once said to me, "Dr. White loved the simple folks out here and visited with us often. He took great pride in seeing his faithful little flowers grow and blossom in the southern Wake County soil."

Elsie Riley: Recalling Willow Springs Service Center

Some of this recollection was collected by me on my many visits to Willow Springs Service Center. Mrs. Riley said, "I sell grocery items and drinks to shoppers while the farmers congregate early in the morning and again at night during the growing season." Hours differed the rest of the year. Besides the Riley's grocery store/service station, there was a barber shop, a beauty shop, a grill, a small shrub nursery business and a fertilizer business, all within the confines of the service center building. Mrs. Riley said, "I open the grill at 5 a.m. where I make the day's biscuits, (two pans full of about 50 biscuits), then I go to the store to open that at 5:45 a.m." Mrs. Riley was one busy woman. Sadly, the Rileys (Leroy and Elsie) are both gone now but this small piece of their lives still remains with me. Mrs. Riley once told me, "Folks around here are just crazy. When a little snow comes our way, everyone wants to have a full tank of gas and two loaves of bread. Where do they think they are going, and is bread all they eat?"

"Life in Willow Springs," an article appearing in the Raleigh times December 26, 1983 provided some of the above information. [77]

Ruth Kinton: Life in Willow Springs

This information was collected during my interview on March 18,

2015. Mrs. Kinton was born right here in Willow Springs in 1928. She was 86 at the time of this interview. Her parents were Mr. and Mrs. J. R. Callis Sr. Ruth was one of the younger children. Some of the older siblings came with their parents to Willow Springs to begin tobacco farming all over again because the "Granville Wilt" ruined much of the land in Granville and other surrounding counties. I asked Ruth to tell me all she knew about the unknown woman buried at Willow Springs Primitive Baptist Church. All she could remember was that "somebody knew more than they were telling about that woman's death. But you know they did not investigate like they do now days."

Our conversation drifted over to Olive's Cash store. Ruth remembered that he was from Apex and operated the store for a long time. He had no children and married late in life. In remembering Hoke Stephens, Ruth recalled he used to be the one to throw the mail bag onto a box car as the train moved slowly by his store on its way to take the mail to its next destination. The tracks were close to the store. Ruth said it was a shame that those train tracks are seldom used any more. She recalled when the Willow Spring Presbyterian Church burned in 1945. She said someone had gone down to the church to raise the heat in the old woodstove that sat in the middle of the main meeting room. The stove pipe going up to the ceiling and attic got too hot and started the fire. The building was an old wood store. It did not take long to burn to the ground. A new brick church was soon built on that property with the help of the Granville Presbytery and the local folks. Ruth and husband, John Kinton, were the first couple to get married there in the new church.

In her book, Kelly Lally documents "The Granville Wilt" as a bacterial disease that stunted the growth of bright leaf tobacco on Granville County's course sandy soil. This forced a few Granville farmers to look to Wake County for better soil and better production."[78]

William E. Callis: Wild panthers, Families, and Crop Failures

Mr. Callis said, "As I made my way delivering the mail, I can remember people telling me of hearing the growls of an animal, probably a panther. It was the great black panther who may have been living along the banks of Panther Lake." He said folks told him they would venture out from time to time to investigate the growls but were never brave enough to walk along the banks of the lake or its branches at night to get a closer look. He also said he remembered the stories of the "Beast of Bladenboro." He thought that too was a panther and maybe the same one that moved up our way. William Callis delivered United States mail and great conversations to our house and others along Bud Lipscomb Road daily. He said "Folks out here in Willow Springs are friendly but not overbearing. They mind their own business and you are free to mind yours.

Callis said his wife (Ann Rowland) and her family have been in the area since her ancestors got a land grant from the King of England about 1700. His family came to Willow Springs about 1915 to grow good tobacco in the rich, sandy soil. William recalled many people came to Willow Springs from 1910-1917 because the Granville County crops were failing. This was probably the tobacco disease called "Granville Wilt" or Black Shank."

Both were due in part to over-production of tobacco year after year on the same land. The principle of crop rotation was known at this time but few farmers practiced it until the crop failures occurred. Mr. Callis said there was a railroad depot in downtown Willow Springs. It was a busy place, especially when folks came to the monthly meeting of the Willow Springs Primitive Baptist Church for the all day long preaching service with their famous "dinner on the grounds." Folks also arrived in Willow Springs by rail to hunt and fish in the nearby resort of Myatt's Mill Pond. According to Mr. Callis, the resort provided cabins to rent for overnight stays. Still more people used the rail service to visit the healing waters of the springs in Fuquay Springs. The last passenger service by rail was discontinued in the 1930s. The depot structure was sold to Mr. Callis and was used as a tobacco packhouse for a short time and was later torn down. Mr. Callis said some of the timbers were used in building a house for his daughter. This writer remembers the old depot when it was used as a tobacco pack house. Some of the old signs were still hanging from the walls and fading as time marched by. In an article appearing in the newspaper, Mr. Callis recalled preacher T. Floyd Adams telling him that willows grew behind the Willow Springs Primitive Baptist Church and were watered by a free-flowing spring. Now that church and that spring are both dried up. Willow Springs Primitive Baptist Church closed its doors 2018. The spring or springs are just a wet spot in the ground.[79]

Cathan (Cathy) Smith Tally:

Remembering her Great Aunt Charlotte Gabrilla Myatt Dove:

While visiting with my friends Cathy Tally and husband Jerry; it soon became clear on me that Cathy had a wealth of knowledge about my beloved Willow Springs. Her family, the Myatts, date back two centuries. Our conversation finally settled into talking about her relatives. Here is but a small part of that wonderful afternoon visit.

Cathy recalled her Great Aunt, Charlotte Gabrilla Myatt Dove, taught school at Southern Side School. That school was closed in 1927. Her Aunt did not go to the new school to teach. According to information from a staff member of the Olivia Raney Library, the Southern Side school building was erected around 1914, to replace an earlier school which had burned in the Middle Creek School District Six in 1899. Parts of the Middle Creek School District became part of Panther Branch School District about 1930. This school was in use until the late 1920s when Willow Springs Elementary School was built in 1926. The record showed that the two-room school closed about 1924.

As we continued to talk about Willow Springs, I remembered seeing an account of Gabrilla Dove when she joined Fellowship Presbyterian Church as one of the original charter members. Charlotte Gabrilla Dove appears on the charter list (October 26, 1913) as documented on church register page 32 and page 20. She was the daughter of Malincia C. Dove and Daniel Peter Dove. Gabrilla was about 21 years old at the time of the charter list. She lived on Barbour Store Road near the intersection of Bud Lipscomb road. The foundation pillars of the old Dove home place are still visible. Gabrilla died in the 1962. She is buried at Mount Pleasant Church. Her grave marker reads:

"Dove, Gabrilla C. born August 26, 1892 died October 4, 1962."

Miss Gabrilla also owned and operated a general merchandise store along Bud Lipscomb Road at or near post station 2081. Today, very little remains of her store venture. Miss Dove applied and received telephone service to her residence in 1955. This information is from the Fuquay Springs telephone directory at Fuquay–Varina history museum. Miss Dove never married. Her father tried to provide a means of livelihood for his unwed daughter through the little store. Cathan recalled most of Miss Grabrilla's brothers received farms at their father's death. As our conversation drifted from subject to subject, it was centered around Cathan's ancestors, the Myatts. Her uncle Albert Winstead Dove's name came up. She recalled that Uncle Winstead and his wife Betty attended a dinner at the North Carolina State Fair honoring families in North Carolina who have lived and farmed on the family land for at least 100 years. His twenty-two-acre farm can be traced back to the original land grant of King George. This honor for Winstead Dove was written by LuAn Jones of the "News and Observer," October 1975.

Carrie and Stamey Mclean's Grocery:

This little mom and pop operation was tucked away just at the intersection of Bud Lipscomb Road and Kennebec Road, a stone's throw from the present-day Fellowship Baptist Church. The old store is now gone—I would assume torn down in the name of progress. The little store had only one gas pump for regular gas only. You could pump your own but always under the watchful eye of Ms. Carrie. The Mcleans lived just across the road from the store. Mrs. Carrie could make that 50-yard dash in record time when nature called. Mrs. Mclean had free range chickens at her house. For the chickens it was a fearful run from the hen-house across the road to the Fellowship Baptist Church Cemetery. Many did not make it and became roadkill. I suspect those chickens faithfully attended every funeral. The Mcleans were truly a lovely couple and I miss them greatly. They always had time for conversation. The gas was cheap, the advice was free, and the conversation was priceless. Our son Patrick was a regular at the store during those hot summer days of working in tobacco under the watchful eye of Bobby Harvell. The McLeans sold an array of groceries and snacks but always in limited quantity. They had hoop cheese by the slice cut to order from a large hoop. I was their best cheese customer. The store operated for many years at that location and upon Mr. Stamey's death the store finally closed in 1993. I am sorry for the newcomers to our area. That little store was right in the middle of everything that is going on now.

Mrs. Eva Pollard: Nails in the Road Bed:

"In the late 1800s, the road that went from the Stage Road to Willow Springs was called the Tram Road. It followed what is now Panther Lake Road until it came to the farm where Julian Pearce now lives. It then crossed behind where his house is and between where Edith Crabtree and Larry Adams now live. The road came out at Barker's store in downtown Willow Springs. The road was straightened in the 1930s and came out where it now goes by the Primitive Baptist Church. However, some people continued to use the old part of the road as a shortcut. Someone purchased the farm behind where the Adams family now lives and decided to close the road. People kept taking down the new owner's barriers and using the road whenever they wanted to, so he took drastic action and sprinkled the road with roofing nails. A car drove to Willow Springs by way of the shortcut and, on the way back, it ran over the nails and punctured all four tires. This almost caused the only Willow Springs local family feud. Not long after that, folks got the message and no longer used that shortcut. Parts of that old roadbed are visible today if you look for it carefully." This story was first told by Mrs. Eva Pollard to Julian Pearce.[80]

Julian Pearce: That Old Oak Tree and Joe "by God" Fish:

Julian Pearce tells the story of a neighbor whose name was Mr. "By God" Joe Fish. Mr. Fish was 12 years old in 1880 when he rode his horse to Ella Fish's home and tied his horse to a small oak tree in front of the house. The horse nibbled the leaves of the tree. At that time the house was a two-room structure. It was enlarged and remodeled over the years, and this same house is where Wade Pearce, Julian's son, now lives, and the huge oak tree is now at least 15 feet around. We estimate this tree to be approximately 125 years old. I am not sure why Mr. Fish had the words "By God" in his name, but sometimes a phrase like that might suggest Mr. Fish was always right or at least he thought he was. I inspected that oak tree recently and it is truly an old one. I included this recollection as I think it adds a little flavor and maybe a little polish to an almost forgotten story and precious memory gem. [81]

Mrs. Ila Myatt Dupree: Life in 1908 around Willow Springs

This information is recounted from a taped interview this writer had with Mrs. Ila Myatt Dupree at her home on February 10, 1979. Mrs. Dupree was born March 13, 1898 and died March 13, 1984. Her husband (Mr. Arley Dupree) was present during the interview but did not talk much. Taped interviews are an interesting way to collect data from first recall. Often this data can be flawed by a person's recollections. Mrs. Ila told me her mind plays tricks on her from time to time. I found her to be on the mark when it came to things happening back "there and then." She was a delightful lady—always polite. I never heard a bad thing about her from anyone, but her manner of speech did let me know very quickly what she was thinking. I never saw her without her hair formed into a ball on the back of her neck. She was short in stature but long in wisdom.

Most folks are reluctant at first to talk freely while you hold a microphone in their faces, but after a while, Mrs. Ila began to talk freely, especially if the right questions were asked-. She provided me with much information. In any event, it was fun to have conversations with folks who have such a wealth of information. This kind of information can only come from a leisurely face-to-face conversation between two friends. That is how I thought of Mrs. Ila. My question to her was, "Tell me about your first days of going to a proper school?" According to Mrs. Ila Dupree, she did go to a proper school. The proper name of the school was Harvell, being named after the Harvells and also because it is located near the old Harvell graveyard. All the evidence collected to date clearly indicates there was first a school at post station 1749 on Bud Lipscomb Road beginning about 1903 until about 1913. Shortly after the school closed a Presbyterian church was located on the same site.

Mrs. Dupree further stated that she recollected attending the school at Harvell or Griffis School when she was five years old. Mrs. Dupree was 81 years old and was born in 1898. This would place her at the Harvell/Griffis school as early as 1903. She attended school again at Harvell/Griffis school at age 8. No reason was given as why she skipped 3 years between school years. Recently, I have obtained a picture of the students at Southernside School, and Mrs. Ila Dupree is there. I have a list of the students by name. I am uncertain as to the date I have guessed the date of the picture to be about 1908. She was identified as Ila Myatt at that time.

According to Mrs. Dupree, her father didn't like the teacher who was working at Cannon Grove School located near the Ogburn farm along Old Stage Road. Consequently, her father, who was a Myatt, had all his children moved back to the Harvell/Griffis School. According to Mrs. Dupree there was a great movement of people into the area about 1910. Mrs. Dupree also remembers tobacco farming coming to this area. She recalled a man named Spivey. She could not remember his first name. Mr. Spivey came to Wake County from Granville County. He purchased the land next to Mrs. Dupree's father (his last name was Myatt). Mr. Spivey is buried at Fellowship Baptist Church. Mrs. Dupree recalls Spivey well because she said he looked just like George Washington. Mrs. Ila said she did not like this old man and could not remember why. When he died, Mrs. Dupree was 14 and she got out of picking cotton all that day to go to his funeral. This happened about 68 years ago according to Ms. Ila Dupree. This would make the year 1910-11. This is not intended to be an absolute correct order of events but does reflect her thoughts to my questions. At first, she was shy to answer questions into a machine but, as the interview proceeded, she opened up, and the things she shared are priceless gems. She helped me polish up many of those almost lost memories.

Mr. Whales Blalock and his wife: Life around Willow Springs

Many people may not remember Mr. Blalock. He and his lovely wife came to Fellowship early in its Baptist days (1962). They were neighbors of Jim and Joy Aycock, the first pastor of Fellowship Baptist Church. The Aycocks and the Blalocks both lived in Fuquay-Varina. The Blalocks were members of Wake Chapel Church at the time. They joined Fellowship Baptist Church to help with the Sunday School program. They quickly endeared themselves to the people at Fellowship and were loved by the church membership. Mr. Blalock said 1909 is certainly the correct year when he attended school at Harvell Griffis School. According to Mr. Whales Blalock, his earliest recollection of Harvell School was in the year 1909. He said the name of the school was Griffis and was named after his grandmother. Mr. Blalock was also sure his grandmother Eveline Griffis gave the land for the school and later for the Presbyterian Church. The principal and only teacher at Griffis School was Mr. Will Peak. Mr. Blalock remembers when Dr. White (pastor of First Presbyterian Church in Raleigh) came to his mother for permission to build a church. His mother, Ritty Anne Griffis Blalock, granted that deed and, for some reason, Ms. Griffis or Dr. White failed to record this deed, so within the last 20 years Mr. Blalock and his sister Aline Fish and other heirs signed a deed for the Church.

This interview was conducted in February 1979. According to Mr. Blalock his earliest recollection of tobacco in the area was the crop in 1910. Mr. Blalock remembers that year because a black man named Mr. Young Smith came to see his mother about renting the farm. Mr. Smith stated that he planned to raise tobacco on the place. Mrs. Ritty Ann Griffis told him she had no barns on the land to store his crop nor any money with which to build barns. Before 1910 the only crops raised in this area were corn and cotton.

I cannot locate Mr. Blalock in the picture of Southern Side School but he was right about the teacher, Mr. Will Peak. According to Mr. Whales, as I knew him, the land on which the old plank church was built belonged to his grandmother, Mrs. Eveline Griffis. Ms. Griffis donated the land originally for the building of the school located at the same site. Mrs. Eveline Griffis and her husband Josh are buried at the Layton Fish homeplace. According to Mr. Blalock, in 1912, a Dr. White, probably from the First Presbyterian Church of Raleigh, approached his mother, Mrs. Ritty Ann Griffis with the proposition to redesign the property and build a church on the land. I think that at this time the school was no longer operating as a school. The old school building was still there but not in use as a school and probably in need of much repair.

The original school had conflicting names. According to Mr. Blalock, the school was called Griffis School, being named after his grandmother Eveline Griffis Blalock. According to Mrs. Ila

Dupree confirmed that the proper name for the school was Harvell. It is not important at this time to determine which one was the proper name for the school. The important fact here is that Fellowship Church, Presbyterian first and later Baptist, started at the site of this school.

Sometime prior to 1912, the school was no longer needed because a new school had been built a little to the south of the Harvell/Griffis site. The name of this new school was Southern Side School. This school was built with the parents raising half of the money and the county/state providing the rest of the money. This concept was called "subscription schools" and was used in Wake County to allow for school buildings and teachers paid for by a partnership between the parents and the state. This school, named Southern Side, is presently located by traveling north from our present church and turning right on James Austin road leading toward the Arlis and Tera Reaves' home. At the time of the writing of this project (2021), the school was still standing and is located in the field near Sandra Myatt's House. I am not totally convinced this is the original site of the school. Often schools were moved around the area and were used for farm storage. In a more recent interview with Lewis Dupree, he stated that Southern Side has always been located just where it is now.

According to Mr. Whales Blalock, one of the games played at the Harvell School was called "Pin the backs to the wall." The object of this game was to have all the strong boys just push all the weak boys against the wall and hold them there until they got away or the teacher made them stop. Mr. Blalock said there were about 60 students attending the School in 1909/10.

As far as the construction of the church is concerned the plank school located on the site had been torn down or perhaps altered for another purpose, prior to the raising of the new church structure in 1915. It is possible the material from the old school was used to build the new church as nothing was wasted in those days and traces of other old school structures have been located in the area.

According to both Blalock and Dupree the front part of the church was built about 1914 or 1915, and the addition of the back part of the church consisted mainly of two large rooms that were added about 1938-39. Mr. Blalock remembered helping with the construction of that addition. It is important to remember that the front part of the church with the stained-glass windows was built first in 1915 under the direction and organization of Dr. White, and his home mission board members of the First Presbyterian Church of Raleigh. Getting all these gems of information was a great day for me.

Chapter Ten – Remembering Some Special Chores

Putting up

"Putting up" or canning peas, peppers, and pickles were essential tasks to ensure there would be food during those cold winter days and nights. Back in the good old days before electricity was available, folks found ways to preserve the food long after the harvest. These old-fashioned methods came to America with the early settlers or were practices used by the Native Americans. Two hundred years ago, whether you came from a family of great wealth with slaves and servants or a person of very little means, the same techniques were used to preserve your food. Brandy Warlick has recorded several stories of her memories relating to food preservation. This was necessary because there was no reliable back-up plan. A quick trip to the local supermarket was out of the question. Before the canning process came into full use, canneries were operating in school cafeterias during the summer months, always under watchful eyes of the North Carolina Department of Agriculture and Jane McKennon (State Home Demonstration Agent). Successful canning became a popular process of preservation. Until the early 1960's, there were still parts of Willow Springs that had no electricity. I can remember when I came to Willow Springs back in 1963, Miss Susie Adams and her sisters did not have electricity at their house in the Mount Pleasant area. I am told 50% of all attempts to can food for extended use failed. Folks just did not understand the process of pasteurization. Dirty jars and lids were the guilty culprits. Salt, smoke, and dehydration were also popular methods of preserving food.

Sulfuring, Fumigating or Bleaching Apples

This story of sulfuring, fumigating or bleaching apples was an old preservation process. The author of this story is unknown. The story that was told to Mrs. Warlick goes something like this. "The old folks would cut up and peel a tub of horse apples. (Horse apples is a loose term referring to any tree fruit such as apples, peaches, and pairs and generally used for animal consumption). After the apples are peeled and thinly cut, they were placed in a tub. A little sulfur in a saucer is set in the tub, a match is struck, and the burning sulfur in a saucer is placed with the apples in the tub. The whole thing is covered and allowed to burn out. You could use the bleached apples all winter and up into May and they would still be just as crisp as the day you preserved them." [82]

In their book, K. Todd Johnson and Elizabeth Reid Murray recorded this account of churning butter:

"All young girls, especially on farms, knew something of the science of and labor involved in converting milk to butter. Gladys Baker of Wakefield (up in the Northeast corner of Wake County) described the processes she learned in the 1910s. Fresh milk straight from the cow was strained into a wide shallow pan. After the cream rose to the top it was skimmed off and put into the churn. All of this at the right split second and at exactly the right temperature. Then the work began. With the up and down motion of the churn paddle you churned and you churned and you churned some more until the butter came. The next step was to scoop the butter out of the churn with a wide bowl. You would then pour the rest of the milk and buttermilk back into the churn with water. It was tempting to drain the water into the slop bucket (where the food scraps were kept for the hogs) but one learned quickly it was better to use another container to avoid the fatal error of accidently dropping butter into the slops. When the butter came out creamy your work was considered a success."

After all these processes were completed the butter was shaped into a small ball. The butter ball was pressed into a mold with a design. I remember the imprint of a daisy was common."[83]

Eloise Smith: Drying apples

Eloise Smith (Mrs. Henry Smith) from Willow Springs had a different plan to preserve her apples. The apples were peeled and sliced thin and were placed on a wire screen. She put a mesh net over the apples to keep the flies out. The whole thing was placed in the sun for a few days until the thinly sliced apples were dry. She stored the apples in a clean white pillow case and hung it in the dark pantry of her house. I can still remember the smell of those wonderful apples. Eloise (my mother-in-law) started a family tradition of making fried apple jacks on the morning of the first measured snowfall each winter. Every family member knew when the time was right. We all came about the same time for a visit to talk about the snow and, of course, to enjoy those apple jacks. I do not know how many she made, but we never ran out. I know all this first hand as I was a son-in-law in that fried apple jacks family.

Harold Newton: Killing Hogs and Curing Hams

Much like the "corn shucking social events" held throughout the South, the "hog killings" were also a social event. Not only did it gather people to help with the combined intensive labor, but the end product was fresh meat for many farm families. Also, equally important, was the opportunity for folks to get together to talk, laugh, and exchange the news of the communities.

"Early Wake County farmers raised a variety of livestock; swine, beef cattle, sheep and poultry. Swine was one of the most common. Wake County farmers allowed their livestock to roam free during the spring, summer and early autumn. Foraging on acorns and other mast in the forests fattened the animals at no cost to the farmer. Colonial farmers identified their hogs by cropping the animal's ears in a certain design. The earmark designs were registered with the county courts should ownership disputes occur. Disputes in Wake County were rare."[84]

Harold Newton from Willow Springs was my ole fishing buddy. He told me this story of curing pork meat. He said:

"Five days after the first frost of fall, folks would pick out the hogs to be killed that year. They were shut up in small pens and fed only corn. The corn got the pigs cleaned out real good and also made the meat taste better. When the weather started getting colder, folks had hog killings with several families pitching in to do the work. Often as many as twenty animals were killed at one time. The hogs were first shot in the head. It was best not to let the hogs see the gun as that may cause the hog to stress resulting in tough meat. The animal was then hung up by its back legs onto a gallows made especially for the occasion. A cut was made to the throat allowing the hog to bleed out quickly. While the hog was still hanging, a straight cut was made from head to tail along the under belly. When this was done correctly the internal organs were removed while still encased in the membrane that held them. This also helped the blood to drain out quickly. The poor hog was then dipped into a vat of hot water (170 degrees) and the hair was scraped away. If the water was allowed to rise higher, it would cook the meat ruining the process. The liver and heart were saved; the intestines were removed and cleaned for chitlins.

The head was removed to be made into hogshead cheese or some other delicacies. The head contained many choice parts. The remaining body was cut in five sections: two hams, two shoulders, and the back bone with ribs attached. The back bone contained the pork chops and tenderloin. Some of the tenderloins were cut away and taken to the main house. There they were cut into pieces, battered, and fried providing a great breakfast treat for all the workers. Of course, the lady of the house cooked a fresh pan of biscuits to add to the treat. This special treat was part of the reward for their labors and was served with large pots of hot coffee, and Grandma's homemade fig preserves. The tenderloin was a prime cut and a real treat to all. Remember, this all had to be done on a special day when temperatures were just around freezing, too cold and the salt would not "take" (properly cure the meat). If it was too warm, the meat would spoil.

Old folks said you never kill hogs on the filling of the moon as you cannot bleed the animal correctly. When the moon is tilted, it is called a spilling moon and makes for better hog killings. The hams, shoulders, and other choice parts are taken to the smoke house where they are laid on a clean slab of wood with a liberal amount of salt on the board. Salt is then poured over the ham and worked in the meat leaving no opening for insect to get in. The most feared insects are the "skippers" who get into meat and lay eggs therein. After several weeks in the cold smoke house, the salt is dusted away and a liberal amount of black pepper is added. Some folks mix the salt with brown sugar."

The shoulders and side meat were done the same way. All the meat was hooked and hung by wire hooks to keep mice away. Six to eight weeks later, when the meat was dry and no drippings were visible on the smoke house floor, it was time to cut a ham. Harold said the best way to cut the meat was about middle way up the ham at the thickest part, removing about a pound of the cured meat. If you had skippers, you could see them right away. After a short cry over all that wasted time and work, you knew the entire ham was ruined. It was removed from the smoke house and buried at least twenty feet from the other meats.

You may be wondering why this section of hog killing has been so long. You see Harold told me all these stories while waiting for the fish to bite. As I recall, we had lots of time on our hands. Harold was a good story teller. I only wish I had written more down. When the fish were biting, we brought home many fish. On trips when the fish were not biting, I brought home many stories and good memories.

Edith and Zoe Stephenson: Collecting Peanuts

This story comes to me from Edith Stephenson and husband Zoe, my old friends back in Varina. She said they saved peanuts in early winter by pulling up the entire vine and, after a good washing in the nearby creek, the vines along with their roots containing the nuts were placed on top of a tin shed. There they stayed for weeks until thoroughly dried. The nuts were pulled away from the roots and were saved in a pillow case hanging somewhere away from the winter rains. On cold, long, winter nights, the nuts, still in their shells, were placed on the hot surface of a wood stove and were parched. Those roasted nuts made for a great midnight snack along with some good ghost stories.

Dougles Honeycutt: Tater Hills

This story comes to me from Douglas Honeycutt, my uncle. He lived out on one of the many Judd farms near Varina. He said root vegetables such as sweet potatoes and Irish potatoes were harvested (dug) in the fall of the year after the green vine started to die down. The tator hole was dug about three feet in the ground. A layer of clean pine straw was put down and the potatoes were placed in the hole. Small Pine trees were cut and laid over the hole covering it. More pine straw was added to the top. This allowed the temperature inside the hole to remain a constant 56 degrees. When potatoes were needed, the smallest family member opened the "tator hole" from the south side and crawled in far enough to pick up the needed potatoes. When leaving the hole, great care was taken to close the opening with much pine straw. If entry to the hole was made from the north side, it might let the potatoes freeze.

Telfair Smith: All about Chitlins

This story comes to me from Telfair Smith and is based on an interview I had with him back in October 1982. According to Mr. Telfair, hog killings were not a part of the true barter system, but neighbors often worked together to kill several hogs at one time and in one location. It was always done in the winter as refrigeration was a problem. The ideal temperature was 36 degrees: any warmer risked the meat spoiling and any colder, the meat would not take the salt properly.

Mr. Telfair Smith, an old friend and member of Fellowship Baptist Church told me once he and Mrs. Inez, his wife, would help folks kill hogs. They often received a mess of chitlins and some cuts of the meat for their labors. Mr. Telfair said he always made Inez clean those hog guts as he could not stand the smell. Inez would wash the guts through several waters carefully turning the guts inside out. The final cleaning was a series of slinging the long guts around and around until any matter (bits of corn) on the inside had been slung out. I am not sure I understand all Mr. Smith was telling me here. I have listened to his tape several times and that's what it sounded like to me. I can just see Mrs. Smith slinging those chitlins round and around while Mr. Telfair held his nose.

Bryant Tyndall: Sweet Pickles

Pickling has always amazed me. How can you put salt on cucumbers and they turn out to be sweet? The secret, I was told, was to use enough salt. "How much is enough," was my immediate question. The answer, so I was told, is enough to float an egg in a five-gallon stone crock. Sure enough, after three weeks in the salt, the cucumbers are ready. After their weeks in the salty brine, nothing can spoil them. Salt that can float an egg is the key. Alum will turn the flabby cucumbers into crisp pickles. Vinegar, sugar, and spices make the cucumbers sweet. It is all truly magic.

Corn Shucking

With the mechanization of farm equipment around Willow Springs and North Carolina much of the fun of farm life was removed. Corn shucking was the one big exception.

"Each autumn, farmers would take turns holding the corn shuckings. The invited guests were neighbors. They were expecting an invitation as it was a time for labor sharing. Better still it was a time for social mingling. Conversation ranged from politics to just some good juicy neighborhood gossip. Religion was off the table. The days preceding the corn shucking event the farmer was busy piling the dried corn from the storage barns into long rows head high and sixty foot long. The farmer's wife was also busy readying the evening supper for many people. The events were usually planned around a full moon. In later times electrical light were strung in the barnyard. The tables needed for all that food were made from planks placed on sawhorses also placed in the barnyard. With several quart jars of moonshine hidden half way down the pile, folks doing the shucking knew a party was soon to follow. Young and old alike shucked the corn for each other. The young boys liked to find those rare ears of red corn. According to custom when found the lucky boy got to kiss the girl of his choice. Nothing was ever said about her luck. A good shucker would grab an ear of corn with his right hand, twist off the husk with a snap of his wrist and fling the shucked ear straight out in front of him dropping the husk behind him.

Nothing was wasted because the husks were fed to the hogs. Some folks saved the husk to stuff a mattress, making a soft warm bed on those cold winter nights. The whole shucking process took only a few hours and then it was time for supper. Someone would always have a fiddle along and the music soon started up. The surprise was the quart jars of corn liquor hidden somewhere in the piles of corn. That always made for good shucking and even better dancing. The barn raisings, the quilting bees, the candy pullings have also become a thing of the past. Corn shucking is still hanging on." The information was in part taken from the book by Roy G. Taylor, Sharecroppers: the way we really were. [85]

Mary Honeycutt Stokes: Feed Sack Fashion

No stories of the life in early Willow Springs could be complete without a feed bag fashion show. Cotton bags became a source of fabric for clothing in the early twentieth century. These feed bags became so popular they soon replaced wooden barrels as containers. Chicken mash, hog feed, and flour were often purchased for the patterns on the bag as much as the contents.

LuAnn Jones writer of Momma Learned us to Work explains on page 172 of her book. Jones suggests "During the 1920s, clothing made from cotton bags became an emblem of poverty, a testament to ingenuity, and a badge of pride to the wearer." Contests were staged and patterns were made available for dresses, table coverings, window curtains, and underwear all from the cotton feed sacks. The first steps in transforming these 1 and ¾ yards of material into use was to remove the durable inks that emblazoned them with colorful brand names and company logos. This was indeed a formable task. First you must dissolve Octagon soap and Red Devil lye in warm water. Soak the bags overnight. The next day you boil the bags. Next step was to rub them on a washboard. Then soak in Clorox and at last you have a plain cotton bag and when cut along the seam line yielding about two yards of material. Local dyes made from walnut husk or sumac berries added the colors.

This feed bag fashion story was told to me by Mary Gladys Honeycutt Stokes about her sister, Lizzie Mae Honeycutt. According to Mary, Lizzie was quite the looker in the early 1930s. On one occasion, she had a date with a long sought-after beau (boyfriend). She immediately started on a new flour sack frock to impress her new catch. She worked on the dress for several days and thinking she would always wear her new frock with a sweater she omitted the formable task of removing the colorful brand name from the bags. The story told to me was that Lizzie and her new beau strolled hand in hand down the streets of Duncan on a warm Sunday afternoon. Feeling a little warm in that sweater Lizzie removed it. There on the backside of her lovely creation were the words in bold print "self-rising guaranteed."

Mary Allene Turlington Honeycutt: Recollecting Earlier Times

My thanks go out to Mary Turlington Honeycutt in writing down some of her early memories in her book, Remembering the Past. While Mary's stories were in a setting to the east of us in the Coats area, I am sure some of her stories were similar to those of the Willow Springs folks. Mary talked about the high ceilings and the cold winter nights in her childhood house. She spoke of how warm a feather bed could be on those cold winter nights. Mary said "her bedroom was cold in the winter and the fireplaces only took the chill out of the rooms. But crawling in those feather beds was wonderful. When you were snuggled down in a thick feather bed, you would be as warm as toast." [86]

Everything done on those early farms served at least two purposes. In the case of the geese, they ate the grass and bugs in the fields and gardens. They also provided feathers for pillows and beds. According to Mrs. Honeycutt's account, the harvesting of the feathers must have been quite a process. It was done once a year in the fall. The geese-picking days were always damp and rainy because feathers didn't fly away on that kind of day. The geese were taken by the feet with the head was tucked under the arm, and the picking began. The collection of feathers was stuffed into a bag and dried on every sunny day for a month or so. Mary talks about sharing the pillows with folks burned out or anyone just getting married. I can't help feeling a little sorry for those poor geese as it must have been a painful process. I sure hope those feathers grew back before winter set in. I wonder what the SPCA would say about this today. [87]

Geese, guinea fowl, and peacocks were often used by the farmers to warn of approaching danger from owls, hawks, fox, and other critters of the night with two legs or four and intending to have a good barnyard supper.

Gail Amos Woolard & Bryant Tyndall:
The Day a Bank Robber Came to Varina

Not much out of the ordinary happened around Varina for most of the year. July, 1957 proved to be an exception. It started as just another hot summer afternoon in Varina when news came from the Crown Station (now property of CVS pharmacy) which was run by Milton Lanier (often referred to as the "Glory Hole") that a bank robber had robbed the First Citizens Bank in Angier and was on his way to Varina. Very shortly after that news, the stolen car driven by Worth Whitaker crashed into a retainer wall at the Varina residence of Flora and Sam Amos (Gail's parents). Gail saw and heard the crash. Mr. Whitaker jumped from the crashed car and ran south down main street. Now you would think with an armed robber coming to your town everyone would be heading the other way. Not so for Gale Amos and her childhood friend who wanted to see a real bank robber up close and personal. The intrepid pair reached the ice plant on Main Street located near the First Methodist Church just in time to become eyewitnesses. Gail recalled Pete Tyndall was drawing upon Whitaker with his gun. Gail remembers Tyndall's clear yell for the robber to stop. Whitaker continued to walk. Tyndall fired his weapon striking Whitaker in the jaw. Tyndall then arrested Whitaker.

He was first transported to Dr. Crumpler's office in Fuquay Springs where he was treated. Whitaker was then transported and jailed in Raleigh. Whitaker did have a weapon when arrested. Later a trial was held, Whitaker pleaded guilty and was sentenced for his crime. Gail remembers the talk around Varina was "Pete had shot a bank robber." I too remember that day. Officer W. T. Tyndall (Pete) was my Dad. I was about fifteen years old, and on that day, some of the North Street boys were about to gather at

Thomas's Drug store for ice cream treats when news broke of the bank robbery in Angier. The robber was headed to Fuquay where he had left a second get-away car. News traveled fast. Soon the entire town was on alert and nervously waiting the robber's next move. I knew my father, a policeman for the town of Fuquay Springs, was on duty that very afternoon. I returned home to share the news with my mother where we waited for more information. The robber, Worth Whitaker, fled in a stolen car from the scene of the Angier robbery and headed to Fuquay. One of the tellers at the Angier Bank followed Whitaker to Varina and made the call to the "glory hole" alerting everyone of the impending danger.

Accounts are not clear why Mr. Whitaker abandoned the stolen car and was on foot (Perhaps the car was inoperative). As he walked at a fast pace south around the curve at the ice plant, my dad, Officer Tyndall, walked slowly north with weapon drawn along Main Street. He then fired his weapon striking Whitaker in the face. Eyewitnesses in the area recall sparks in the air, followed by the sight of blood on the robber's jaw. Ironically, my father had never fired the gun prior to this event. My dad was a hero; he protected the town as was expected of any police officer. The Mayor and Town Manager came to see Dad offering their congratulations on behalf of a grateful town.

For several days after the event our little house was filled with people congratulating Dad. He got many cards and letters thanking him. Dad was humbled by the event and did not speak of it much. I too was proud of my dad. In the days and months following the event, life returned to its usual slow Varina pace. After serving some time for his crime, Whitaker returned to Garner, his hometown. After his return, Dad and Whitaker connected. Whitaker offered his apologies. Dad accepted and they both moved on with their lives.

Gail has some great memories of her life in Varina and freely shares them with everyone. She remembered Varina as a child-friendly place to live, explore, and ride her bicycle. Her childhood memories of Varina also reflect my memories.

Gail married Dale Woolard. Several years later they were out to lunch at the "Toot-n-Tell It" in Garner when Dale pointed out Worth Whitaker, the bank robber, also having lunch. Gail recalls the scar on the side of Whitaker's jaw. Thanks to Gail and her friend for arriving at the right place just in time to become eyewitnesses to some real history of my beloved Varina. Just a few days after the robbery, Dad received a letter from J. Edgar Hoover, Director of the Federal Bureau of Investigation, Washington D. C., thanking Dad for his work in connection with the case involving Worth Alexander Whitaker and the robbery. Director Hoover further wrote: "The splendid assistance rendered by Officer Tyndall merits the deep appreciation of the personnel of this Bureau and I want to take this opportunity to commend you on your outstanding performance of duty."[88]

Chapter Eleven- Remembering Strange Events

Not only did the good folks of Varina and Willow Springs remember special people, special places, and special chores, they also told me stories of strange events such as the mysteries, murders, mayhem, and missing persons right here in Willow Springs and Varina. Every community has at least one of these stories and someone gifted to tell them. Varina and Willow Springs are no exception.

Before I start to write this portion of my recollections, let me ask you clearly and up front some questions. Are there such things as ghost? Are there haunted places on this earth? Are there portals on this earth where the spirits can move freely in and out? Does the orb of a deceased person remain on earth for a while after the physical death? Is there something to all that paranormal research being conducted at Duke University?

Places where great tragedies occurred such as Bentonville battle ground in North Carolina have been the sight of recent ghost sightings (see "News and Observer" November 5, 1990). What other evil deeds has the prince of darkness thought up for us to endure as he is tramping around his grounds at Harpers Crossroads in Chatham County? This story in its entirety is North Carolina's best known scary legend (see "News and Observer" article by Josh Shaffer). It would be nice to have an answer to all these questions, but I just do not know. When it comes to telling ghost stories, the spirit that sometimes enters these stories is just a term used to denote something yet to be explained and has nothing to do with my religious beliefs. I can easily separate the two. I hope you are also able to do this. [89]

My childhood was rich with classic tales of dark, moonless nights long, long ago, far, far away and sounds that go bump in the night. Tales about a spirit deer or spirit bears appearing all make for great story telling and even greater entertainment. It is the entertainment factor and storytelling skills that appeal to me. Somewhere between facts, fantasies, and drama is the truth about ghosts and the spirit world. I just love to tell the stories. High drama adds a little excitement, and I like doing high drama. You must choose which are proven facts and which are just made up. I love to make them as scary as possible just for the entertainment value.

Lewis Dupree—Lights at the Graveyard:

I am a storyteller and ghost stories make for great storytelling. I am sure the only things in the cemetery at Fellowship Baptist Church are dirt, head stones, a few fire ants, and bones for right now. None of them are moving around with the exception of the fire ants. As for ghost stories, they always occur on a dark, moonless night and almost always near a graveyard. That is the setting for this story. I heard this story many years ago. A couple of versions of this story, all with the same ending, have been told and retold over the years. For now, it is just fun to include them in this my collection. After all, some believe what you are about to read did occur right here under my beloved Willows. Both Fred Fish and Lewis Dupree have said they too have heard versions of this story. Here is what I have pieced together over the years.

It seems around the turn of the 20th century, let's say about June 4, 1915, many peddlers came to our area selling an assortment of items. One man in particular sold fresh fish from his horse-drawn wagon. He usually visited Willow Springs on Fridays. For some reason, that is always a great day to sell, buy, and eat fish. This peddler, (I think his name was Williams), was in our area very late one Friday evening. He and all the other peddlers knew that the hairpin curve at the Fellowship Presbyterian church cemetery was not a good place to be after dark. It made the horses jittery and hard to control. It was as if they knew or saw something we did not know or see.

In any event, Mr. Williams had a great day selling many fish and was very late leaving our area to head back to his home in Fuquay Springs. Rather than take the long, safe route home, he chose the short cut, going by the cemetery at Fellowship Church. It was dark and, of course, moonless. Just as he was making the turn into the curve, his horses began to rear up as they tried to free themselves from their harnesses. At the peak of the confusion, a light moved slowly from the cemetery to the horses, holding them still in their tracks. Mr. Williams said the light was so bright in the cemetery you could read the newspaper by it. The light stationed itself between the horses and was only a few feet from Mr. Williams. The light assured Mr. Williams he had nothing to fear.

The light further signaled to Mr. Williams this would be the last time he would ever see the light. I am not sure, but I do not think Mr. Williams believed the light. The light told him that on this very night, it had gotten the thing it had been waiting for all these years and now would leave forever. Mr. Williams, frozen with fear, asked no questions but proceeded with great urgency to Fuquay Springs, his home and safety. Later Mr. Williams heard that a man from Willow Springs was found in his home dead. The time and date of the death was June 4, 1915. Could the light have been waiting for this man? Was the light a good or bad omen? No one will ever know for sure. Since that time there have been no further lights appearing in the church cemetery. This story ends here leaving many paranormal questions remaining.

The Mysterious Death of a Beloved Grandmother During WWII

This story comes to me from a dear friend, Mrs. Vaughn Phillips, back in Varina. She was a great storyteller and I hung on her every word as her stories unfolded. The story over the years has several versions but the outcome is still the same. It seems that during World War II, somewhere in Germany around 1943, a young American soldier found himself surrounded by the enemy and out of bullets. The night was dark and he was afraid. It was just a matter of time before he would be killed as the German enemy advanced toward him with guns blazing. At that moment he prayed to God for forgiveness of his sins and prepared to die. His thoughts turned to home in what he believed to be his last minutes on earth.

His beloved grandmother, back in North Carolina, appeared to him in a clear white vision. She said to him," Stand up my beloved grandson and follow me." As he did, he walked past the German guards. They could not see him. Just as he made his way to safety the German guards began to fire their weapons again. The date was April 4, 1943 about midnight. As was common in times of war, the news traveled slowly. Several weeks after his miraculous escape, he received the sad news. His beloved grandmother had been fatally shot in her yard back in North Carolina. She was last seen by family members around midnight standing with her arms held up and her head facing heaven. The date was April 4, 1943. In North Carolina an investigation was conducted and it was concluded the woman had died of gunshot wounds from a German style gun. The family and community were in shock and disbelief. This just could not be in North Carolina. There was at least one American soldier who knew the truth. Can a spirit being travel great distances over great oceans? Anything is possible in the spirit world.

The Legend of Old Barclay Inn:

Many years ago, Barclay Inn was one of the stopovers on the old stage line from Raleigh to Fayetteville. The story is told that two wealthy looking, and well-dressed men stopped by the Inn for a night's rest. When the two failed to show up for breakfast the next morning, the innkeeper mustered up the courage and knocked, then entered their room. There he found one of the men dead, lying on the floor in a pool of blood with a knife in his back. There was no identification on the man. The second man disappeared with no trace. They buried the man in the old graveyard located nearby. They say to this day, you can see the stain of the red blood on the floor. Everything has been tried to remove it, but to no avail.

A few years ago, while reading a later book about the history of Angier (More Voices of Yesteryear, page 361), I read an account by Flonnie Rambeau of a strange happening occurring while she and her family lived in the old Barclay House, circa 1906. Here is a brief account of that story.

"Late one night a noise was heard from the second floor. The sound was so loud her mother just knew something large had fallen. Then came a terrible sound. Flonnie, frozen with fear, spent a restless night waiting for the crack of dawn. The event upset the family so much that they moved back to Angier the very next day." Could that event have something to do with the murder that happened at the Old Barclay Inn all those many years earlier?" I guess we will never know for sure. [90]

The Cowmire Murders:

Again, a very special thanks to Mrs. Edith Pearce and Ruth Hardman for sharing their collections of Willow Springs Histories and stories. Mrs. Edith Pearce, tells this story which came from Ruth Hardman. Ruth was told the account by William David Dupree in 1972. I also got parts of my story from K. Todd Johnson and Elizabeth Murray's book and Pearce & Hardman history notes "the cow mire murders." [91]

My story, coupled with these accounts, goes something like this.

Around the year of 1870, Scott Partin, a resident of Panther Branch Township, married and built a small cabin near his parents along

Black Creek swamp in Panther Branch Township (Wake County). That area is at the end of Bill Love Road. Today (1982) the road is a dead-end dirt path just off Carlie Adams Road. That general area is also the site of an old black water cypress swamp, the result of the damming of Myatt's Mill pond to provide waterpower to a gristmill. Scott Partin's marriage and his ability to pay his debts were both on rocky ground. The couple did have a baby. The young Mrs. Partin had taken the baby to a neighbor for a visit when her husband came for them, He told Mrs. Partin they were going away for a visit to her folks. The two of them left with their baby. Mrs. Partin and child were never seen alive again. After a few weeks the neighbors began asking questions of Mr. Partin. His answer was always the same: his wife and child were visiting her folks. When her folks came asking about her whereabouts Scott had also disappeared. His brother told the Waltons (Mrs. Partin's folks) that they had all slipped away to escape debts that Scott was unable to pay. He said the family had moved to Goldsboro. The brother was believable and the story was forgotten. When a traveler to Goldsboro returned with news that the Partins hadn't been seen or heard from down there, the Willow Springs folks again begin to worry. Suspicion continued to mount and a search was conducted around the area of their cabin and surrounding swamp lands.

According to Billy Ray Yeargan, my new friend from Angier, the exact location of the cabins is not known today. The site is somewhere near the end of Bill Love Road where there was a quagmire. This was a place where the mud was almost like quicksand. During times of extreme rainfall, the area had standing water colored a dark red from the tannic acid in leaf decay. When the men neared this spot, they smelled carrion. The strong odor caused the search party to concentrate on the quagmire. Scott's father told the searchers the odor was a decomposing cow. Again, the Partin's story was believable and the searchers moved to another area to search. After searching fruitlessly for some time, the men in the search party decided to return to the quagmire since this was still the most likely spot for the disposal of the woman and child if they had met a brutal death at the hands of someone. This time the men saw a bit of cloth and pulled it out. It proved to be Mrs. Partin's bonnet. The men then searched more diligently and eventually turned up several parts of human remains, possibly Mrs. Partin's body. The body had been dismembered with an axe or knife, then bagged and buried deep into the boggy quagmire. The dead cow was almost the perfect way to hide a body and odor. The Partin baby was never found and Scott Partin never returned to Willow Springs. The community was left only to guess what other dark deeds went on at the Partin cabin. What other blood was on the hands of Scott Partin?"

Could the mysterious light in the Harvell cemetery (later known as the Fellowship Presbyterian church cemetery) that dark moonless night be for the life of Scott Partin? I do not know if Scott Partin ever faced justice for his alleged crime. I do know Little Black Creek swamp does exist and, on my visit, I did see an area of bog land with red tannin water covering much of it. Sorry to report I did not see a body or any of the parts. Several years later a man mistaken for Scott Partin was jailed in Raleigh. Later evidence proved it was a case of mistaken identity. The man was identified as Robert Leson Porter. He was said to have stayed in Raleigh several months after being released from jail until he was summoned to return to his native country, where he said he was to inherit a large estate.

Further research has revealed Albert Partin, a Blacksmith by trade was father to Scott. Albert also had two other sons, John Henry Partin (also a blacksmith) and George Partin. Albert Partin operated what was known then as the Hurley Dupree Mill. That mill is just downstream below Myatts Mill on Black Creek. DNA testing could help solve this mystery. But it was not available in 1875. No further sightings of Scott were ever made. Scott's Father and brothers continued to live in the area of Willow Springs. It was described as the crime of the century which remains unsolved. Law enforcement authorities in Wake, Johnson and Harnett counties tried for a number of years to bring to justice the alleged perpetrator of one of the county's most heinous crimes ever.

Evidence indicated that Albert W. (Scott) Partin, Jr., a native of Ireland, murdered his pregnant wife Anna Walton Partin and one year old son in February 1875 in Panther Branch Township. After attempting to burn the bodies, he dismembered them with an axe and knife, he placed the parts in a guano sack, and buried the remains in a nearby quagmire in Little Black Creek Swamp. He threw a cow's carcass on top to repel searchers, but the scattered body parts were finally discovered in June 1875. By then Partin had fled. His father and two brothers were arrested as accomplices but were soon released. Sightings of Scott Partin were reported when Governor C. H. Brogden offered a $400 reward from the state for his capture, supplemented by another $400 from local residents. Community leaders, James A. Adams and Dr. J. T. Leach, called a mass meeting of the citizens from the three-county area to aid in the search for the killer. In spite of all efforts however he was never apprehended. Local officials thought they had a break in the case in 1888, when an Irishman resembling Partin was jailed in Raleigh. He had handwriting and scars similar to Partin's and could not tell a straight tale about himself. Panther Branch area witnesses declared it was a case of mistaken identity. Stories circulated over the years that he settled in Florida, Virginia or Arkansas. He was last reported seen in the local vicinity about 1913." Both the "News and Observer" and The Fuquay Varina Independent wrote accounts of this crime.[92]

It is possible that someday someone may be walking along Black Creek and out of the mist of a foggy morning a pale image may appear, rising out of the swampy water. In a low mournful voice, Anna Walton Partin cries out "justice for me and my babies." Anything is possible in my spirit world.

Mystery of the Big Panther

My land of the Willows is full of mysteries. As I said earlier, most ghost stories happen on dark moonless nights. That setting in itself is scary enough, but when you add to it that something coming out of a dark swamp making blood-curdling cries, it strikes fear in all and elevates the degree of horror. It always makes for great story telling. Back in 1953 there were reports of a monster, half cat and half man, who was eating dogs and goats in Bladen County. The town folks of Bladenboro called the animal the "Beast of Bladenboro." The nervous town chewed its collective fingernails in daylight hours and dreaded the pitch of night. Afterwards an article in the Wilmington Morning Star, October 29, 2006 (Wilmington's newspaper), documented the account of mysterious killings of animals. Something was then sucking the blood from the bodies, leaving only the flat, dry skin. With the town in fear the stories took on a life of their own. The more the story was told the greater it grew. I have always liked mysteries like that one.

Back in 1953, I was working at the Varina Theater selling popcorn. Nessie Oliver who sold movie tickets, loved to talk to me about the "Beast of Bladenboro." With wide eyes and a little fear, she said there was a large black cat (perhaps a panther) living in Willow Springs. I believed her story, but like so many of my quests, it was put on the back burner. It was not until 1969 when William Callis, my mail carrier, told me he too had heard the stories about the Willow Springs monster. He said he was told by several folks that Willow Springs had a monster of its own. Callis recalled the big cat came out only at night. He reminded me that I need not travel 90 miles southeast to encounter a bear-like coyote panther. Mr. Callis said "This could be where Panther Lake and Panther Branch got their names." Could the unseen, but often heard, blood curdling growls along the lakeshore be the one and only Willow Springs monster? There was never a sure sighting of the beast. You can be the judge. An account of Bigfoot sightings around Littleton, North Carolina, near Lake Gaston, continues to be reported resulting in a museum of artifacts relating to this Chewbacca.[93]

You can be your own judge, but as for me, William Callis, Nessie Oliver, and grandma, "we believe."

In my research on the Bladenboro monster incident, I found another article written this time by Josh Shaffer of the "News and Observer."[94] Shaffer commented how "The little sleepy town of Bladenboro had cashed in on its monster fame. Each November they have a "Beastfest" to celebrate the monster. The city has concluded that the blood-sucking animal while feeding off fear did bring money to a needed part of eastern North Carolina."

I was just thinking the folks in Willow Springs, could have a weekend to celebrate along with collard sandwiches. Mrs. Elsie Riley and the folks at BB's grill might sell beast burgers or panther pies. Maybe someone could tell ghost stories along the banks of Panther Lake or at the Willow Springs Primitive Baptist Church cemetery. That would be a perfect job for me.

Alas, I think we have waited too late to implement these money-making ideas. For sure, there are strange things out here. In October 2019, someone reported seeing a real live coyote trotting along Old Stage Road. A few years back, black bears were reported to have a den along Kennebec Road. Brandon Gardner, grandson of Jim and Maxine Gardner, saw this animal up close and not too comfortable. The N&O (March 29, 2016) reported a bobcat citing along the Haw River in Chatham County. Legends of a monster-like snake in the Catawba River date back for centuries and some cite proof of it as seen in a new grainy photo taken over at Sunset Point picnic area on Lake Wylie. ("News and Observer," December 31, 2019) There is still time for the reappearance of black panthers and other crawling monsters in the night here under my little Willows. Plan your midnight strolls along our lake shores carefully and always watch where you step.

"In 1764 Panthers, wolves and other vermin were so common in this dark corner of what was to become southern Wake County, a reward was offered. The head of the vermin was taken to the County courthouse (Joel Lane's Traven) as proof." Elizabeth Reid Murray comments on these events in her book, Wake A Capital

County of North Carolina Volume I. [95]

Chapter Twelve - Remembering the Oddities

There is so much I have learned, loved, and laughed about in my Willow Springs and Varina stories. Like any other place in this old world, there are strange things going on all the time. Some are to be explained and others forever to be a mystery. Willow Springs and Varina are no exception. For lack of a better word, I call them my little oddities and I accept them for what they are. Part of the joy of living out here and back in Varina is that you just have to embrace with a big grin your life in these places. Some things are never going to change.

You also have to be very careful what you say and to whom you say it. It seems almost everyone, at least in Willow Springs, is kin somehow. A good example is Maxine Adams Gardner who had 23 first cousins, but she was an only child. Ray Bowden had 29 cousins, but he had only one brother.

I thought those numbers were impressive until Judy (my wife) and I were talking about large families when it suddenly dawned on us that she had 31 first cousins. The story gets even more convoluted when you consider this; Judy has one full brother (Glenn), one half-brother (Michael), one full sister (Linda Lee), one half-sister (Retha Ann), three step sisters (Melba, Patricia, and Nancy), and two step brothers Joel and Dwight). I am pretty sure if we look back further, we are going to find a quarter horse somewhere.

Over all these many years I have tried to be a good historian. I have been serious and diligent in my research and collecting skills. I have been careful to never judge and to always listen. I have tried to separate facts from fiction, often in the middle of fragmented stories, missing memories, and fading recollections. Many of these odd facts are still covered in the dimming dust of time. Still many more are patiently waiting for someone to pick them up and polish them off and have a little private laugh. After a while, it all gets funny as norms fade into eccentricities. From the very beginning, I did not want this collection and writing project to become a dull chronological, genealogical, or historical account of people and events all under zip codes 27526 and 27592. I thought I would just share a few of these oddities about Willow Springs and Varina. There are many more, but for now, I'll just choose these few to share with you. You may have more oddities of your own, and I would love to hear them.

Before we start down this winding road of the oddities, there is one more piece of the puzzle to lay out here. People have funny ways of saying things. It is not the accent. There is no doubt it is southern as we all are Southerners. I think it is the choice of words we use:

- While talking with Mrs. Vernon Honeycutt (Marie) she once said to me "When leaving a room, we were always reminded to cut out the light." How do you do that, Mrs. Honeycutt? Do you use a saw or a knife!

- Laura Lee Adams once told me to be a successful gardener you must put a one-dollar plant in a ten-dollar hole and always on a wet day.

- Harold Newton said to me when speaking of a person with lots of money," He has enough money to burn a wet mule."

- My good friend, Donald Cotton, over in Varina added to that by saying "yes and in a twenty mile-an-hour wind."

- Sue Holland, our good friend, would say of a person trying to stay true to a difficult situation, "You have to hang in there like a hair in a biscuit."

- Sue also has a cure for almost everything. She said to put a bar of soap between the bed sheets to prevent leg cramps. An onion tied to the foot of the bed will break a fever.

- A person not looking too good can be explained as "death chewing on a nab."

- Mrs. Inez Smith, a dear friend of our family, once said that when describing a person who was not very pretty, she would say the person is "hard favored."

- While still on the subject of beauty it was once said that a man from Varina was so ugly he could "stop a clock or back a bull dog out of a meat truck."

- Folks often say you can not get lost out here because "all roads lead to Cleveland School."

- Daisy Lipscomb once said the best way to shine your shoes was to rub them with a cold biscuit.

- Once Danny Holland was giving road directions to a lady who was not from here and wanted to go to Angier. Danny said, "You take James Austin Road down to the intersection, then take Wimberly Road on into Angier." The lady politely replied, "After taking those roads will I need to bring them back?"

- When describing someone being very mean one might say he is mean as "Blalock's Bull."

- Once while romantically parking in their favorite parking place, probably "the pines." a young Willow Springs lady said to her boyfriend "Aren't the stars numerous tonight," and he, wanting to impress the young lady with his vast vocabulary, replied, "Yeah, and there is a lot of them."

- The wind blew so hard back in Varina during "Hurricane Hazel," it took two men to hold a bed sheet over a knot hole.

I better stop here. This stuff could go on forever. Let's get on to the oddities.

Oddity One: What the heck is the name of this place? To the newcomers, it is Willow Spring, without an "s." When questioned about this, the newcomer's just say, "Well, look at the post office name." To those of us past age fifty who have lived around these parts for many years, it is, and will forever be, Willow Springs with the "s" attached. I just cannot say Willow Spring; it does not roll off my tongue easy. You even might say it leaves a bad taste in your mouth.

On a recent trip (January 2018) down to our local post office to get this matter settled once and for all, I asked, "When, why, and who changed the name to Willow Spring?" The answer I got was sharp, short, and stern "We have not changed the name. It has always been Willow Spring." I thought for a moment and, not wanting to start an argument, I said: "If that is correct, I am guessing the folks over at the elementary school less than forty feet from the post office door did not get the memo. The sign reads "Willow Springs Elementary School."

I really don't care what the Post Office says. However, I will accept the post office's word on this argument. After all, they are our only organized government presence in these parts, and the government always knows what is right and best for us! Right?

In defense of my friends down at the post office, a few days later, I checked the application as far back as 1898 for the establishment of a Post Office for Willow Springs down at the Fuquay-Varina Museum. I found an application from T. R. Temple for a Post Office.[96] It was Willow Spring, no "s." That sort of took the wind out of my sails. I still insist that it is futile to tell that to some of us old timers. According to findings in Wikipedia November 15, 2015, they write: "There is only one natural spring in Willow Spring, which is why it is called Willow Spring instead of Willow Springs." [97] If that is true, just when did the other springs dry up around here? Fuquay has springs as does Holly Springs. So, why not us? Somewhere in the middle of this mess there is an answer. I just may run out of time on this earth before I find it. Lately, someone else advanced the theory that the name change to Willow Spring was due to the recent droughts and global warming. I think I will just leave that theory alone completely. Still, someone else told me the name just had to be changed as there were too many places called Willow Springs in North Carolina and it was confusing to those global position systems and that big satellite in the sky.[98]

Oddity Two: As if things are not already confusing enough, there is another place here under my little Willows in southern Wake County. The second Willow Springs community is located just ten miles to the east in Johnston County. This is according to the U.S. Geological Survey. That second Willow Springs has a Clayton zip code. Some folks had no idea there were two Willow Springs.

According to some of the older families from the Johnston County side of the region along White Memorial Church Road, that whole area was known as Willow Springs. Today the only visible reminder of that fading memory in the Johnston County Willow Springs is the Willow Springs Free Will Baptist Church, which sits near the official location of the Johnston County community. What happened to that community? Did it just up and leave? [99] The "North Carolina Gazetteer," the Bible of state geography, makes no mention of it.

Oddity Three: Another example of this strange place is our cemetery. Where else can you find a cemetery right in front of a school? But such is the case with our beloved Willow Springs Elementary School. Some of my wife's third grade students believed it was where they buried the teachers when they got tired of talking or just died. In fact, it is the Allen Family Cemetery. The Allen family owned land near the present school that was built in 1926. Most of the Allen descendants have now moved from this area. It must be comforting to those dearly departed Allens to know that all those little children come to the Allen's graveyard almost every day. According to an article appearing in the newspaper, "Tom and Sarah S. Allen were farmers who came to Willow Springs from Granville County in 1914 so they could raise better tobacco. Their home on SR 2753 faced what was then a two-room schoolhouse. When the new school was built in 1926 the Allens continued to use the family burial ground. There are tombstones at the graves of Joseph C. Allen, a two-month-old infant who died in 1941; Corina Olivia Bullock, who died in 1921; William T. Allen, who died in 1927 and his wife, Sarah S. Allen who died in 1924." There are supposed to be five other unmarked graves in the cemetery. Could they be some of those worn-out teachers?[100]

Oddity Four: Exactly where is downtown Willow Springs? Is it those few businesses currently fronting along highway 42 including Willow Springs Service Center and Polly's Curtains, or is it along Kennebec Road as it curves left out to 401? Is it along

Dwight Rowland Road as it passes the new school and post office? Could it just not exist at all? From my research, I have deduced that the downtown Willow Springs did exist along Dwight Rowland Road (as it is known now) as it returns to Highway 42. The first business of any size was a general merchandise store built by Jim Rowland on the west side of the railroad track about 1912. A. F. Smith and W. B. Temple both owned and operated stores along that stretch of land. The Temple store was converted into Willow Springs Presbyterian Church circa 1914 and burned in 1945. A brick church was rebuilt on the same property. In 1961, that church was later merged with the New Hope Presbyterian Church. In its heyday, downtown Willow Springs had a post office, a depot, a doctor's office (Dr. C.F. Dowd), a blacksmith shop, and several residential houses. All of those are now but a fading memory. Each passing year reduces these sweet memories more and more. I would like to thank Ruth Hardman and Edith Pearce for providing some of this information. They have been a great source to me in preserving these memories. When the road was paved in 1948 changes were made to produce a straight road. This action dried up the downtown along Dwight Rowland Road. Downtown is out there somewhere just waiting for more discoveries to be found.

Oddity Five: What about the mysterious Cannon Grove? Only a few people know anything about these conflicting stories. Often, I hear stories just too hard to believe, but every now and then a story comes along that is too good to ignore and demands to be written down. Is Cannon Grove the site of a plantation somewhere around these Willows? Is it a collection point for low grade iron ore used in the Civil War to make cannonballs? Is it the name of a plantation once visited by William Tryon, the hated colonial Governor of the colony of the Carolinas? Is it the site of a Church or an old school? There is a state highway directional sign at the intersection of highway 210 and Old Stage Road pointing to Cannon Grove 8 miles west. If you follow the sign you will be about where the Honeycutt Landing Subdivision is now located on Old Stage Road. Only in Willow Springs can you lose an entire site. The highway road sign is still there (2019). Check it out the next time you are going down the Old Stage Road.

I checked with the good folks at North Carolina Department of Transportation and sure enough there was Cannon Grove just off Old Stage Road on your left just after Barbour Store Road and just before Bud Lipscomb Road. The 1936 map clearly showed it. The 1944 map did not show it at all. It also did not appear on the older maps of Southern Wake County circa 1930. An old deed recorded before 1900 referenced both Cannon Grove Church and School. Ms. Edna Ogburn remembered some of this story. Footnote to this mystery; I talked to folks at NCDOT; they provided the mapping resource. SR 106 is Old Stage Road. SR 2758 is Bud Lipscomb and SR 2759 is Barbour Store Road. I bookmarked this as a favorite site on my home computer. This information has been given to me over the years with several versions. Thanks also to James and Fred Fish.[101]

Oddity Six: Panther Branch Township is a township without a town. How could that be? In 1868, for political reasons and to better oversee taxing, the county commissioners divided the county into sixteen tax districts later known as townships. Those early county commissioners felt certain towns would soon spring up within this dark corner of the county. Wake County fully expected an economic boom following those bloody years of the Civil War and the period of reconstruction that followed. There was no boom, and there are no towns. Along with the other oddities, this does not strike me as unusual. It is just another of those Willow Springs things you learn to accept. The best we could do was to muster up the unincorporated communities of Willow Springs, Myatt's Mill, and Mount Pleasant. Just another oddity of life here in my land of the Willows.[102]

Oddity Seven: Next we have the story of the Old Jolly Place, our own underground story. Yet another example of odd things going on in Willow Springs. This information was given to me by Doris Griffis' brother, George Stephenson. George is now 89 years old (2017) and living in Smithfield, N.C. He recalled a house somewhere on Bud Lipscomb Road with a large cavern 12 foot down. He discovered this while helping dig a well on that property. He recalls the well was near the house known as the Jolly Place. George said the site was large enough to stand in and some water in it. No one else saw this but George because he was the only one willing to go down that well in a bucket. He was 12 years old at the time. We will just have to take George's word on that one.

The Jolly name comes from a family living along Bud Lipscomb Road. Mr. Stephenson also recalled that just behind the Jolly house there was also a graveyard. Many of the tombstones were tall and the cemetery held the remains of several of the Jolly family members. Mr. Stephenson said the graveyard is now gone, and he does not recall what happened to it. Recently, while telling the story of the underground cavern, Fred Fish said he also recalled a story much like George's account. Fred also said the cavern was large enough to drive a small tractor into it. He told me that the Jolly house was named for the family living there and that one of the descendants started Jolly's Jewelry Store in Raleigh.

Oddity Eight: Who else could have a tombstone of an unknown woman who died on September 16, 1936? You guessed it!! Willow Springs Primitive Baptist Church Cemetery, smack in the middle of downtown Willow Springs. The long version of this story goes something like this. "On the evening of September 16, a man struck and killed a lady as she was walking along the highway near Willow Springs. For weeks an extensive search was made trying to establish her identity. Her body waited and waited at the Ballentine Funeral Home over in Fuquay Springs. No one ever came forth to claim her. After an extensive search for her identity, the local churches organized a funeral. Many folks were present and the Willow Springs Primitive Baptist Church provided a free gravesite. Her gravesite was the first in that new cemetery. To this day, flowers are sometimes left at her grave. Still, no one has come forth to identify her. I have always thought this story was very sad, and I have also gone to her grave many times just to reflect on her life and this mystery. I could sure use a little more polish here on this broken mirror. After trying to put this story together from several oral accounts and fading memories, I found a copy of the Fuquay Springs Independent from September 25, 1936 about the unknown woman and also a story by Edith Pearce and Ruth Hardman in History of Willow Springs, unpublished 1972. I have recorded both here in these accounts. The byline reads "Unknown Victim of Wreck Buried. All efforts to identify a woman killed by truck near Willow Springs prove fruitless:"

"An unknown woman who died in a strange land was buried Saturday in a country churchyard, and a simple metal marker was placed at her headstone. Her gray coffin and her black shroud trimmed in white and the words of a minister made her funeral as reverent as if she had had relatives and friends to mourn her. Caught in the path of a swerving truck near Willow Springs in the Five Points area; where she was trying to catch a ride. The woman, about fifty, stout and with gray hair, was killed. Efforts to establish her identity proved fruitless and the sandy earth of the cemetery of Willow Springs Primitive Baptist Church, not far from the scene of the accident claimed her body and this haunting mystery. The services had been conducted by Rev. J. C. Lawrence, pastor of Fuquay Springs Presbyterian Church and Fellowship Presbyterian Church.

There have been several inquiries including one from Dunn, North Carolina but none resulting in her identification. However, found on her person were two addresses: Lewis Hazlewood 510 Rutherforton Street, Greenville, South Carolina and Frederick Stuart, 215 Park Avenue, Baltimore, Maryland. Efforts to reach someone at these addresses were fruitless. The woman was standing beside the road when a light truck driven by R. H. Holland of Willow Springs entered from a side road and was struck by a motor express truck driven by I. C. Bradley of 905 Lenoir Street, Raleigh, North Carolina. The Bradley truck swerved off the road and struck the woman. The body was taken by W. J. Ballentine to his funeral home. According to Mr. Ballentine the woman was wearing a flowered print dress, the kind provided by the county government. L. M. Waring, the County Coroner, took up a collection for the funeral as he had done many times in the past. The Willow Springs Primitive Baptist church provided the grave."

There was no mention of who paid for her cement headstone. While discussing this strange story with Ray Bowden on March 10, 2018, he said his grandfather, William Thornton Pollard, made the headstone from cement and scratched the wording into the wet cement with a nail. That grave stone replaced the simple metal ground plate provided by the county. It just reads "'unknown woman, September 1936." Sleep on, my mystery lady. Someone will step forward one day and provide your identity. Edith Pearce and Ruth Hardman recorded a story of the unknown woman much like this. For now, anyone having better polish for this mystery or more information can contact Bryant Tyndall. Don't wait too long; Bryant was eight years old when this writing and collecting project first began, and he is now 79 (January 19, 1941).[103]

Once I raised the question of the "unknown woman" while talking with a Willow Springs woman several years back. Her answer took me by surprise when she said "There are some things out here best to remain a mystery." That raised in my mind more questions than answers. Could someone know more than is being said and written? I have been by this gravesite several times over the years. I have noticed flowers on the grave several times. Time will tell all. Sleep on my unknown friend. You did find a place to rest here under my little Willows and a place in my heart. Who knows? Your life story might make a great movie.

Oddity Nine: Where but in Willow Springs can you find an account of 112 Presbyterians baptized. I am not talking just a little sprinkle of water or soft rub with a "wet one." Oh no; I am talking about going under the water all the way down cold and deep and coming forth as Baptist forever. Well, it happened right here under my little Willows in 1963. Here is a small portion of the story as written by Preston P. Phillips Jr. for The Evangelical Reporter Phillips wrote:

"There's a little church tucked away in the farming area of Eastern North Carolina that, only a few months earlier, was called Fellowship Presbyterian Church. Today, this same Church is named Fellowship Baptist Church. 112 Presbyterians were re-baptized by immersion, many of them had been Presbyterian for life, including two Presbyterian Elders."

What could possibly bring about such a revolution? Fellowship Presbyterian Church was organized originally as a mission church and was grouped with four other mission churches in a "circuit." Over time the circuit was reduced, finally leaving only The Fellowship Presbyterian Church and The Willow Springs Presbyterian Church to share a pastor.

The Granville Presbytery made a generous offer; merge the two churches, and we will build you a new church building. Then you'll be all set to move forward with greater visibility and new hope for the future. The proposal was naturally attractive to the members living in the area of the proposed new church and they all voted in favor of the offer; while Fellowship members did vote in favor the vote was not unanimous. Several of the folks at Fellowship felt the community would be left without a church presence. Divesting their community of a church would not be a good idea for them in spite of all the financial advantages which apparently would come from accepting the Presbytery's proposal. These country folks with their simple faith realized that a church is its people, the ministry, and not a fancy building with a high salaried pastor. Then the unreasonable ultimatum came down hard and firm.

They were told that they no longer had access to any Presbyterian preachers by order of the Presbytery. Still, somehow these people didn't believe the Lord had demanded the closing of this Christian testimony in their community. So, the congregation, led by Elders D. T. Harvell, W. W. Pearce and H. T. Ashley (now all deceased) and perhaps others were determined that if they could not have Presbyterian pastors, they would take any kind that would preach the Bible. For 18 months, they managed to function with pastors from various sources, including ten months under the wise caretaker leadership of a retired Methodist pastor from Apex, Mr. John B. Hurley.

Finally, when it became obvious that the congregation was not going to submit to the Presbytery's proposal, they made another magnanimous offer. They agreed to let the folks have the property on Bud Lipscomb Road if they would leave the Presbytery, give up their interest in the new manse, and take another denominational name. It could be Baptist or Methodist, or something of the sort—but not Presbyterian. It was about this time that they came in contact with a Baptist minister, James O. Aycock. The result was that Fellowship Baptist Church (Independent and Missionary) was created. The first order of business was 112 prospective members all to be received by profession of faith and baptized by immersion. Up they popped, "Presbyterians no more and Baptist forever." [104]

Oddity Ten: This is a selection of odd names, places, and occupations in my beloved Varina. A gentleman by the name of Clarence Hare owned and operated the Varina Barber Shop. Just down the street was the local beauty shop owned and operated by Florence Curl. Do you get the hair and curl part? Among the early post offices in Fuquay Springs was one named Varina.

Oddity Eleven: Recently I visited our local Willow Springs Post Office (February 12, 2020). I wanted to give you an idea as to how large Willow Springs really is. Here is what I found. Currently there are now eleven rural routes with 7000 postal stations. The

Post Office on Dwight Rowland Road also has 778 mail boxes. The Willow Spring postal system covers three counties, at least four townships, and four telephone exchanges (Fuquay-Varina, Benson, Angier and Garner). From its west boundary at highway fifty-five to its east boundary at highway 50, the span between is twenty miles. In 1972 there were only two rural routes with 2,300 rural postal boxes and 200 boxes at the Post Office. Who knew we could be that large in just forty years?

Oddity Twelve: While trying to include all the little communities associated with Varina as I remembered them back in 1952, the community of Needmore was included in that grouping. It struck me as odd that it was called "Needmore." Where could that name have come from? I set out to find an answer the only way I know; asking too many questions. I quickly hit a brick wall; no one seemed to know the answer. My luck changed when I talked to my friend Willa Adcock. Willa grew up in Varina with me but has spent much of her adult life in the Needmore Community. She recalled the following story and suggested this might be the reason for the name.

She said there was a small Mom and Pop grocery store located in that community at the intersection of Hilltop-Needmore Road and Sunset Lake Road. The store owners always ordered their supplies in small quantities probably in an attempt to keep the costs down. When folks would buy a can of beans or any other items, they would say to the store owner, "You are going to need to order some more beans soon." Having just a few items in the whole store, folks started calling the store the "Need More" place. Hence, the community was named Needmore. I recall that community store back in 1951. I rode my bicycle out there often searching for old houses and barns to explore. I think the store was operated by the Thomas family.

Thanks Willa, for remembering one of those little gems.

Oddity Thirteen: Now here is that final oddity, and boy, is it a tangled web. It is related to oddity number nine but I think it deserves a place and a number all its own. It seems that back in 1962, there was a new Baptist Church being formed that would lead a congregation mainly of Presbyterians. That in itself is an oddity. The recommendation to become a Baptist Church came from the Presbyterian membership under the leadership of a caretaker, retired Methodist minister, Rev. John Hurly. That is also odd. To add to the confusion, the first called-minister was a Baptist, Rev. James O. Aycock. At that time, he was employed part time by a Congregational Christian Church called Wentworth in the McCullers area. Do you think we could get any more religions in this mix?

Conclusion

As I prepare to conclude this collecting and writing project, I am torn between two questions. Am I a child of "the here and now" or am I a child of the "there and then?" Looking back has been great fun for me. It has brought me joy and maybe to my readers, a little smile. That is all I ever set out to do. Talking face to face with folks about the bygone days and then writing the things they said has brought me satisfaction of a job well done, but never finished. Those folks were truly the voices of wisdom unfiltered and sincere.

Life in Varina and Willow Springs as it was seventy years ago created a group of people sometimes called "the great generation." These people grew up being self-reliant, looking only to themselves to subsist. They endured the Great Depression, the crash of the stock market, and the dust bowl. They marched off to America's many wars when called and said very little of their war time adventures when they returned. They were forced to rely on themselves with only a little help from their neighbors and family. They were kind people willing to help others when asked but never wanting to interfere in another's private life. It was a time of great struggle and yet a time of great joy as families grew closer. The "there and then" generation produced folks willing to work to fix that which was broken and to move on with life after fixing it.

Back at the beginning of this book I talked about how I got started down this road of discovery. It was my attempt to put together an old broken mirror discovered in an old barn in my home town of Varina. Similarly, this project has allowed me an opportunity to put together pieces of the lives of some of the Willow Springs folks and Varina folks and to polish up some of those missing pieces with the recollections of many folks out here in Willow

Springs and back in Varina. I have searched and polished these shards long enough. Now it is time to stop the chase, put away the polish, and call in the hound dogs. This polishing job is complete. I am satisfied with what I have discovered, and I accept full responsibility for my recollections. Any errors made in recording these recollections are just my mistakes and never intended to deceive. They are a product of my memory which sometimes fails me.

When reflecting back over the days of the "here and now" I am reminded, in today's fast-paced world, that my children and grandchildren have learned to rely not so much on their own ability but on computers and other electronic devices to make their way through this world. My grandchildren know far more today than I could have ever imaged. I am not sure that is a good thing for them but it is their thing and their way.

The good ole days worked for me. However, I must admit indoor plumbing, central heat/air, a big microwave with all the bells and whistles, two cars in the driveway, and a television the size of a barn door are now parts of my life today. I just cannot do without any of these things. Everyone from the "there and then" or the "here and now" must find their own way through these perplexing questions. In the "here and now" age, I am thankful I can choose a religion suited to me. I am thankful for the freedoms and opportunities that have been given to me. I am humbled by the people along the way who gave me good advice on countless subjects. I am proud to be a North Carolinian and an American. As I have said to my children and grandchildren countless times "Aren't we blessed?" Good luck to you while finding your way through your memory journey. "How are we ever going to know which way we want to go if we don't know where we have been?"

About the author

O. Bryant Tyndall is a lifelong resident of Southern Wake County where he's never met a stranger. While working nearly 50 years in State Government, he would often spend his lunch hour at the State Archives Building researching the unusual oddities and hidden treasures of the local area around Willow Springs and Fuquay-Varina. Being an active member and unofficial Church Historian for several decades at Fellowship Baptist Church in Willow Springs, he interviewed many of the elderly patriarchs and matriarchs of the community over a span of 40 years. He is a volunteer tour guide at the Fuquay-Varina Museum and a docent at the North Carolina State Capitol. Because of his extraordinary service to the community and state, in 2014, he was awarded the highest citizen honor by the State of North Carolina— Order of the Long Leaf Pine. Bryant and his wife of more than 50 years, Judy, reside in Willow Springs, NC. He has always had a passion for history and a curiosity for getting to know special places and people.

FOOTNOTES

1 Wake Capital County of North Carolina, by K. Todd Johnson and Elizabeth Reid Murray, volume II, Wake County Government 2008, Appendix A: Population Statistics, 1870-1920 page 703.

2 Johnson & Murray page 699, About Willow Springs.

3 The Historic Architecture of Wake County North Carolina, by Kelly A. Lally, published by Wake County Government 1994, page 379, Bank's Quarter became Willow Springs.

4 The North Carolina Gazette, second edition, William Powell and Michael Hill, University of North Carolina, Press, Chapel Hill 2010, page 568.

5 News and Observer February 28, 2017, Barry Saunders staff writer, observed quote of John Hope Franklin first quoted by Santayana.

6 Quoted by Daniel Boorstin in The American Spirit, by David McCullough, Simon & Schuster 2017, page 105.

7 The Fellowship Presbyterian Church Willow Springs, N.C. Reel Number One, microfiche, containing Church, Sessions and Registers records spanning years 1913-1961.

8 Johnson and Murray page 579 About Varina.

9 A History of Fuquay-Varina by Shirley Mudge Hayes and Shirley Danner Simmons, Apex Printing Company 2009, pages 33-42 & 97-120, John Brown railroad agent and John Mills railroad builder.

10 Hayes & Simmons, pages 26 &121, Fuquay's re-drying plants.

11 Hayes & Simmons, page 97, where were the proper Varina town limits?

12 Hayes & Simmons, pages 33-42 & 98, Ennis Family.

13 Hayes & Simmons, pages 97-120, Business at Durham Street.

14 Hayes & Simmons, pages 97-120, Durham Street.

15 Hayes & Simmons, pages 97-120 East Broad Street to old Cotton Gin.

16 Hayes & Simmons, pages 97-120 and 213, Store fronts along Broad Street, West to East.

17 News and Observer, April 18, 2015, staff writer Josh Shaffer (Love of old places).

18 Quote by Dorothy Spruill Redford in Somerset Homecoming, Doubleday, 1988, page 5. These phrases "the there and the then" and "the here and the now."

19 The Cades Cove Story A. Randolph Shields, Copyright 1977, Preface page ix Errors.

20 Powell & Hill, page 395.

21 Michael Doyle Boyette "Ode to A Tobacco Barn" The Flue Cured Tobacco Farmer 11/3/98.

22 William Faulkner, as quoted in The News & Observer June 14, 2015 by staff writer John David smith, "The past is never dead. It is not even past."

23 Pearl S. Buck, a poet and writer of the twentieth century said "(inside myself is a place where I live all alone and that is where I renew my springs that never dries up)." This quote was taken from the internet February 29, 2020.

24 History of Avery County North Carolina by Horton Cooper, Biltmore Press, page 27, "Where there is life there will be records of people and their lives."

25 Raleigh Times, October 4, 1974, by staff writer, Mary Lee McMillan Johnson's Gardens.

26 Willow Springs Flicker School Year Book 1955 advertisement section, H&H Grill.

27 North Carolina's Tobacco Heritage, published Tobacco Institute 1875 "I" Street Northwest, Washington, DC 2006, pages 14-17, titled "Tobacco price supports and production."

28 MacRae-Brazier Map 1833, North Carolina Division of Archives and History, & Lally, page 9.

29 Lally, Page 9, bad roads.

30 Lally, Introduction Page 5, Indians.

31 Johnson and Murray page 699, About Willow Springs.

32 Edith Pearce and Ruth Holland Hardman wrote A Brief History of Willow Springs, consisting of several type written pages on several subjects, unpublished. 1972, Willow Springs trains.

33 Hayes & Simmons quote by Ruth Johnson page 33, Coming of the railroads.

34 Voices of Yesteryear a History of Angier collected and written by Betty Coats Pleasant, Ruth Summerlin Gregory, and Linwood Alford Matthews 1969, pages 21 & 23, Trains.

35 Pleasant, Gregory, and Matthews, pages 5 & 7, Mr. Williams and Mr. Angier.

36 Lally, page 11, see also post by Willa Adcock, "Mother's Best Christmas." //wwwrighthereinfuquayvarina.com 2014/12/23/ Bad roads.

37 First Steps in North Carolina, Cornelia P. Spencer, pages 72-73, Alfred Williams Co. 1880.

38 A New Voyage to Carolina, London 1709 by John Lawson. Also News & Observer 1/16/74, 2/28/2017 and Winston-Salem Journal 10/15/67, also better known by its second posthumous title The History of Carolina, 1741, (see also footnote # 71)

39 Pearce & Hardman, Old Federal Road.

40 Lally, page 11.

41 Pearce & Hardman, Old Tram Road.

42 Lally, page 397, Old Fayetteville Road.

43 Lally, page 399, Three Creeks Church.

44 Historical Raleigh, Moses Amis, Commercial Printing Co. 1913, pages 287-288.

45 Hayes & Simmons pages 19-25 & www.candidslice.com /love-letters-healing-springs http5/20/2014, & Murray and Johnson page 576.

46 Lally, page 397, the communities in Panther Branch Township.

47 News and Observer Lyn Ragan, Early Land Grants in Southern Wake County and Northern Harnett County, See also lynragan.com.

48 Johnson and Murray page 703.

49 Lally, page 397, slow population growth.

50 Johnson and Murray, page 687, Myatt's Mill.

51 Elizabeth Reid Murray, Capital County Printing Company 1983, pages 22-23, 26 & 102, Volume I, the Myatts, and England to America 1400-1998, David H. Myatt, Accuprint 1998, pages 30, 31 & 63.

52 Murray, page 102, The Myatts England to America 1400-1998, David H. Myatt, Accuprint 1998, pages 30, 31 & 63.

53 News & Observer, October 1975, by staff writer LuAnn Jones, "300 Years Down on the Farm" Winstead Dove, a descendant of the Myatts is honored at NC State Fair and England to America 1400-1998, David H. Myatt, Accuprint 1998, pages 30, 31 and 63.

54 Raleigh Register, and North Carolina State Gazette 7/15, 1834, Mary & Mark Myatt and England to America 1400-1998, David H. Myatt, Accuprint 1998, page 30, 31, & 63.

55 Murray pages 26 & 443, & (Lord Granville's Land Grants, NC State Archives).

56 The Heritage of Wake County, North Carolina,1983 edited by Lynn Belvins and Henriette Riggs, Wake County Genealogical Society, Hunter Publishing Company, Winston-Salem, N.C. Post Office at Myatt's Mill.

57 Sharecroppers: The Way We Really Were, Roy G. Taylor, J-Mark 1984 page 185.

58 News and Observer June 29, 2018, section 7C, Forgiveness", crossword puzzle.

59 Pearce & Hardman, ABC store.

60 Johnson and Murray page 278, The Toddy Tax.

61 The Willow Springs Flicker Year Book, 1957 Advertisement, Francis Mill.

62 Autobiography of Elder T. Floyd Adams, written by his son, pages 17-18.

63 Fuquay-Varina Independent, September 13, 1990, Fellowship Fire.

64 Fuquay-Varina Independent, February 24, 2010, section 1C,

Adams House Fire, as transcribed by Willa Akins Adcock.

65 http//wwwrighthereinfuquayvarina.com Annie Mae Adams Akins 1985, posted by Marguerite Greene, March 10, 2015, & submitted by Willa Adcock. Sherman's March.

66 England to America 1400-1998, David H. Myatt, Accuprint 1998, page 63, Sherman's March.

67 dated 8/12/2012, Submitted by Willa Adcock "Farm Life in Willow Spring", as written by Susie Adams.

68 The Raleigh Times, by Treva Jones 12/26/83 as quoted by Anna Jones Stephen.

69 The Raleigh Times, by Treva Jones 12/26/83 as quoted by Doris Messer.

70 Lally, page 5, Indians.

71 A New Voyage to Carolina, London 1709 by John Lawson. Also News & Observer 1/16/74, 2/28/2017 and Winston-Salem Journal 10/15/67, also better known by its second posthumous title The History of Carolina, 1741, (see also footnote # 38).

72 Mudge & Simmons, Pages 1-3, Indians.

73 First on the Land, Ruth W. Wetmore, John Blair Publisher 1975, Pages 65 & 68-69.

74 Lally, page 5.

75 The Raleigh Times by Treva Jones, December 26, 1983, as quoted by Eula Smith Harris.

76 The Raleigh Times by Treva Jones, December 26, 1983, as quoted by Charles Strickland.

77 The Raleigh Times by Treva Jones, December 26, 1983, quoted by Else Riley.

78 Lally, page 67, Granville Wilt.

79 The Raleigh Times by Treva Jones, December 26, 1983, quoted by William Callis.

80 Pearce & Hardman, story of "nails in the roadbed."

81 Pearce &Hardman, story of Joe "by God" Fish and the old oak tree.

82 Brandy Warlick, Morganton, NC, article on "Food Preservation" Good Old Days Magazine.

83 Johnson and Murray   page 429, Making Butter.

84 Lally, Page 11, Marking Hogs.

85 Taylor, Pages 18-19 and News and Observer November 4, 1951, corn shucking.

86 Remembering the Past Mary Allene Turlington Honeycutt, Work/Shop Press Inc. Atlanta, Ga. 2004, pages 6-7, about high ceilings and warm feather beds.

87 Honeycutt, pages 6-7, about plucking the Goose on wet days.

88 Fuquay-Varina Independent, July 25, 1957 & August 1, 1957, also an online post of December 26, 2018, Fuquay-Varina Museums Historically Speaking, written by Shirley Danner Simmons, "The Bank Robbery recollected by Bryant Tyndall and Gail Amos Woolard." Circa 2019

89 News & Observer November 5, 1990 Bentonville Battlefield.

90 Pleasant, Gregory and Matthews, page 102 Barclay Inn.

91 Johnson and Murray page 356, and Pearce and Hardman Cow Mire Murders.

92 News and Observer, March 29, 1903, March 15-16, 1918, and April 3, 1955, see also Fuquay-Varina Independent November 9, 1983, Cow Mire Murders.

93 News & Observer May 23, 2016, Josh Shaffer writer, Bigfoot, Littleton, N.C.

94 News & Observer 10/14/2018 & Wilmington Morning Star 10/29/2006 Bladenboro Beast.

95 Murray, Vol. 1, page 27, "Bounty on Panthers in Panther Branch Township."

96 Fuquay-Varina Museum copy of an application for a post office, September 22, 1899 at Willow Spring note no "s", W. B. Temple applied and was granted permit.

97 Wikipedia (November 15, 2015), too many "s."

98 The Raleigh Times, by staff writer Treva Jones, December 26, 1983. Willow Springs with or without an "s."

99 News and Observer, January 3, 2005, titled "Identity Fading."

100 The Raleigh Times, by staff writer, Treva Jones, December 26, 1983, "the Allen's graveyard."

101 State Maps N.C. DOT Shelly Health "Cannon Grove."

102 Lally, page 397, Odd fact "township with no town."

103 The Fuquay Springs Independent September 25, 1936, also Pearce & Hardman, Unknown Woman.

104 Preston P. Phillips Jr. Evangelical Presbyterian Reporter "112 Presbyterians become Baptist" February 1963.

If you enjoyed this book, please leave a review so that others may find it.

Made in the USA
Coppell, TX
21 February 2021